P&O-ORIENT LINERS
OF THE 1950s AND 1960s

William H. Miller

AMBERLEY

For Howard Franklin
Cherished friend, loyal P&O passenger, grand ambassador for
all that is British

First published 2014

Amberley Publishing
The Hill, Stroud
Gloucestershire, GL5 4EP

www.amberley-books.com

ISBN 978 1 4456 3813 3 (print)
ISBN 978 1 4456 3830 0 (ebook)

British Library Cataloguing in Publication Data.
A catalogue record for this book is available from the British Library.

Typeset in 11pt on 12pt Sabon LT Std.
Typesetting by Amberley Publishing.
Printed in the UK.

One of P&O-Orient's most beloved and popular liners, the *Arcadia*, in a
dramatic view at sea. (P&O)

CONTENTS

Dedication   2
Foreword   4
Introduction   5
Acknowledgements   6
P&O-Orient Lines – The Fleet   7
1   *Ormonde*   8
2   *Mooltan* and *Maloja*   9
3   *Chitral* and *Ranchi*   11
4   *Orontes*   13
5   *Otranto*   15
6   *Strathnaver* and *Strathaird*   16
7   *Corfu* and *Carthage*   20
8   *Orion*   21
9   *Strathmore*   25
10 *Stratheden*   27

11 *Empire Orwell*   31
12 *Empire Fowey*   33
13 *Canton*   35
14 *Orcades*   37
15 *Himalaya*   42
16 *Chusan*   48
17 *Oronsay*   54
18 *Arcadia*   58
19 *Iberia*   69
20 *Orsova*   72
21 *Cathay* and *Chitral*   77
22 *Oriana*   81
23 *Canberra*   93
Afterword – P&O and Princess Cruises   109
Bibliography   128

FOREWORD

Iconic brands. Household names. In today's world of ubiquitous advertising and global markets, there are dozens of brands which could be universally regarded as such. However, if we hark back to the 1920s and 1930s, or even into the 1950s and 1960s, there would only be a handful of such iconic companies. In the USA, they may have included Ford automobiles, Coca Cola soda and *Time* magazine. In Britain and her Commonwealth countries, there would be Rolls-Royce cars, Cadbury's chocolate and British Petroleum.

Across the British Commonwealth there was one shipping company in particular that also could claim iconic status – P&O (the Peninsular & Oriental Steam Navigation Company, later P&O-Orient) line. While there were, of course, other famous British shipping companies, such as Cunard and British India, none could trigger such wide-ranging recognition as P&O. By virtue of their far-reaching trade and central roles in transporting people and mail throughout most of the Commonwealth, P&O and its ships were household names not only in the UK but also in countries such as Malta, Egypt, India, Singapore, Hong Kong, Australia and New Zealand, and later became well known in the USA, South Africa and Canada.

Many a citizen of the aforementioned countries will recall experiencing one or more of P&O's white liners, either as immigrants setting out for a new life on the other side of the world, as business people or sportsmen and -women on international tours, as tourists taking that once-in-a-lifetime visit to their families' 'old country' (or perhaps on a '*Women's Weekly* World Discovery Tour') or as young people heading off on their first post-university overseas adventure. Others may simply have gazed wistfully at the gleaming ships from the pier as they welcomed relatives or friends or saw them off while throwing colorful paper streamers. Later, many thousands had their first taste of life on a liner on a P&O cruise. P&O initiated cruising from London in 1844 and from Australia in 1932. Years later they entered the US market.

I am honored and delighted that the author, Bill Miller, invited me to write the foreword for this book. Bill ('Mr Ocean Liner') is ideally placed to present the story of this legendary company, thanks to his astonishing experience of passenger ships, new and old, his extensive resources, both personal and photographic, and his skill as probably the most prolific passenger liner author in the world.

Let Bill take you back to a world where grand, white liners with their buff funnels would take you on a regular five-week voyage, teak decks would be freshly scrubbed each morning ready for promenading and shuffleboard, and Goanese stewards would graciously serve bouillon on deck at 10 a.m.

Tim Noble
Melbourne, Australia
Summer 2014

INTRODUCTION

It was a magical June afternoon in 1962 – blue skies, big, puffy clouds and crystal-like clarity. The great Manhattan skyline was glistening and gleaming. It was just after lunch, several of the great Atlantic liners had sailed past while outbound for Europe and, just beyond, the big Bethlehem Steel shipyard seemed almost crowded with ships under repair. Tugs and barges and floating cranes shuttled about, of course, and were the 'supporting cast' in the ongoing maritime production that was then New York harbor. I had a special purpose on that day, however. Not just a new liner was arriving, but a unique liner. P&O's stunning, very modern flagship *Canberra* was arriving on her first visit. Gradually, I could hear the booming whistles echoing from farther downriver. These were the salutes between other ships, harbor craft and the *Canberra*. Finally, the sparkling white hull of the 818-foot-long liner appeared from behind the sheds of local piers and a small shipyard that repaired tugboats. Once in full view, the *Canberra* – with her raked bow, tucked-away-on-a-lower-deck lifeboats and yellow uptakes placed aft – looked magnificent. She was, every inch of her, a superbly designed ship and very much a great hint of the future. I stared and stared, a flotilla of Moran tugs escorting the liner as she slowly moved along the Hudson. She would berth at Pier 90, the Cunard terminal at the bottom of West 50th Street and best known as the berth of the *Queen Mary* and *Queen Elizabeth*. The *Canberra*, on a cruise from Southampton to New York, would be at berth for seventy-two hours, serving as a hotel for her 1,700 passengers (her cruise capacity was specially reduced from the maximum of 2,272 passengers).

Previously, I had only seen two P&O liners, part of the merged P&O-Orient Lines family that I knew only from collecting brochures gathered at Cunard's very grand headquarters in Lower Manhattan, at 25 Broadway. P&O-Orient liners were fascinating, big, diversely routed and said to be the 'Biggest Bloomin' Ships on the Seven Seas'. The *Arcadia* and *Iberia* visited New York in 1959. I saw both of them. They appeared big, powerful, very much the 'great ocean liners'. Previously, in peacetime, P&O's *Stratheden* had made four calls at New York, chartered to Cunard for four crossings, but in 1950. Being only two years old at the time, I 'missed' seeing that Strath liner. Afterward, we had the exciting visits of the revolutionary *Canberra* in the early sixties and, beginning in 1979, several calls by the equally important *Oriana*. A very special visitor was the *Chusan*, which made a one-time call in October 1971 as part of a charter cruise from Cape Town. We had a tour aboard followed by lunch and indeed it was a fascinating glimpse of one of the classic post-war P&O liners.

I was a guest speaker aboard the *Canberra* and *Oriana* from the late seventies and met P&O officers, crew and many loyal passengers. There were tales and recollections reaching back to the 1920s and 1930s of long-ago steamer trips to India, Australia and the Far East.

These days, the era of P&O-Orient liners in the 1950s and 1960s is all but gone, gathered in the pages of maritime history. Happily, P&O Cruises keeps up something of the spirit. But hopefully, this book will be something of a nostalgic voyage – a reminder of many wonderful ships. Myself, I can almost sit back, close my eyes and see, say, the classic-looking *Iberia* sailing from London on a long voyage to Australia and then around the world. Whistles sounding, flags fluttering, passengers lining the decks – yes, run away to sea!

Bill Miller
Secaucus, New Jersey
Summer 2014

ACKNOWLEDGMENTS

The author wishes to thank Amberley Publishing, Stephen Card (for his cover material), Tim Noble (for his Foreword) and Michael Hadgis (for technical support).

Further appreciation to the late Frank Andrews, Nula Bryant, Frank Bucklow, the late J. K. Byass, Captain Nick Carlton, the late David Carr, Michael Cassar, Tom Cassidy, Luis Miguel Correia, the late Alex Duncan, Robert Eldridge, Captain Bob Ellingham, Richard Faber, Ginger Fortin, Howard Franklin, Henry Gibbons, the late John Gillespie, Mick Harper, Clive Harvey, the late Frank Jackson, Captain Philip Jackson, Lindsay Johnson, Elinor Kamath, the late Andrew Kilk, Norman Knebel, Tony Ralph, Captain Martin Reed, James L. Shaw, Ian Spencer and the late Mary Stevens. Added thanks to Moran Towing Co., the Port Authority of New York & New Jersey and most especially to P&O itself.

P&O-ORIENT LINES – THE FLEET

What Cunard was to the Atlantic run, P&O was to Eastern waters – particularly to India and Australia. The company was, in fact, a very important, vital link within the framework of the once mighty British Empire.

P&O could trace its roots to 1837, when – as the Peninsular Steam Navigation Company – it opened a mail service between England and the Iberian peninsula. Three years later, as trading expanded into the eastern Mediterranean, the title was more aptly revised to the Peninsular & Oriental Steam Navigation Company, 'the P&O' for short. Later, as services expanded beyond Suez, the Company's arch-rival, at least out to Australia, was another British firm: the Orient Line. Decades of rival passenger liners of increasing size, speed, comfort and even luxury followed. It was not until 1960 that the two firms were formally – and sensibly – merged, becoming the P&O-Orient Lines (the name reverted to P&O only six years later, in 1966). This union created the largest passenger ship fleet afloat, a distinction maintained for some years thereafter.

P&O had their brand-new flagship *Canberra*, followed by the near-sisters *Arcadia* and *Iberia*, the *Chusan*, *Himalaya*, *Canton*, *Stratheden*, *Strathmore*, *Strathnaver*, *Strathaird*, *Corfu* and *Carthage*. The Orient Line had their fondly dubbed 'O Boats', which included their new flagship *Oriana* as well as the *Orsova*, *Oronsay*, *Orcades*, *Orion* and *Orontes*. Then there were aging pre-war liners, sent into post-war migrant service mostly, and so their service records extended into the first half of the fifties – ships such as the *Ormonde*, *Mooltan*, *Maloja*, *Ranchi* and *Chitral*. Completing the list of the twenty-eight passenger ships covered in this book are two peacetime troopships, managed for the Ministry of Transport: the *Empire Fowey* and *Empire Orwell*.

Beginning in 1954, these P&O and Orient liners began to expand beyond their traditional Australian and Far East sailings: first across the Pacific to the North American West Coast, then completely around the world and, by 1963, even on a transatlantic operation. By the early 1960s, P&O-Orient liners spanned the globe, regularly touching at over 100 ports on five continents.

The transatlantic link, for example, was based at Port Everglades/Fort Lauderdale in Florida, then an expanding liner port. Sailings were arranged in- or outbound from London (or Southampton on the larger *Canberra* and *Oriana*), and usually called en route at Bermuda and/or Nassau. The ships carried Atlantic passengers on these seven- to ten-day segments of their more extended journeys to and from the North American West Coast or direct to/from Australia via Panama. The service was two class, first and tourist, and the fares were attractive and sometimes exceptionally reasonable. As late as 1970, for an eight-day passage between Port Everglades and Southampton in the 29,000-grt *Arcadia*, minimum tourist class rates began at $110.

Over forty years later, but aboard P&O Cruises, passengers can still sail the world – on long, extensive voyages aboard the likes of the *Aurora*, *Ventura*, *Adonia* and the current *Oriana*. The global scope of P&O continues.

1

ORMONDE

Commissioned almost immediately after the end of the First World War, in November 1919, she endured and became Orient Line's oldest passenger ship to resume services after the Second World War.

'My family emigrated to Australia in 1949 and we sailed aboard *Ormonde*, then a very old ship,' remembered Ian Spencer.

We went out on the £10 plan so we were hardly expecting luxury, not even comfort. The ship creaked and rolled on that long voyage, which took, as I recall, about seven weeks to Sydney. We said goodbye to England, our home, on a foggy day from the Tilbury Landing Stage. England seemed to disappear, almost in seconds, as the *Ormonde* moved off and into the Thames. The food was basic, but seemed almost a banquet compared to still heavily rationed Britain. There were large tables in the otherwise dark-colored, very wooden dining room. The cabins were large and crowded – twelve and more to a room. Years later, I visited Britain aboard the *Oronsay* and later the new *Oriana*. They seemed like a century apart from the old *Ormonde*.

The 15,047-grt *Ormonde*, built by the famed shipbuilders John Brown & Co. on the Clyde, sailed on the UK–Australia run until the outbreak of the Second World War, in September 1939. Used as a troopship, she sailed unharmed until 1947, when she was refitted, but for migrant passengers only – a maximum of 1,070 in all.

One of a growing fleet of post-war British migrant ships used on the Australian run, the end for the 600-foot-long *Ormonde* came almost forty years after being launched, in May 1913. The aged ship was decommissioned by P&O in the fall of 1952 and that December she sailed northward to Dalmuir in Scotland to be demolished.

2

MOOLTAN AND *MALOJA*

The very first P&O liners to exceed 20,000 tons, these twin-funnel liners served on the pre-war Indian as well as Australian services. After their wartime duties as armed merchant cruisers and then troopships, they were reconditioned for one-class migrant services. After being restored in a shipyard in the London Docks, the *Maloja* resumed passenger service in June 1947; the *Mooltan*, refitted at Belfast, returned to P&O service two months later, in August. Each ship had been reconfigured to carry 1,050 one-class passengers.

The sisters *Mooltan* and *Maloja* were P&O's biggest liners when they were commissioned a month apart in the fall of 1923. Impressive-looking twin-stackers, they weighed in at 20,800 tons, 625 feet in length and were designed to carry comparatively few passengers for ships of their size, 656 in all (327 in first class, 329 in second class). They were built by another famed shipbuilder, Harland & Wolff Limited of Belfast. The two, twin-screw ships were powered by steam triple-expansion engines, but could make only a rather sluggish 16 knots. They were used on P&O's mainline service between London, the Mediterranean, Suez, Ceylon and then to Australia – to Fremantle, Melbourne and Sydney. Periodically, they also served on the London–Bombay run. Used as troopships during the war, they were returned to P&O in 1947. Beginning in the summer of 1948, they were back on the Australian run, but in low-fare service. Their voyages often included calls at Aden and Colombo; the return sailings sometimes included calls at Bombay to collect British officials, civil servants, workers, their families and troops following Indian independence.

The late Mary Stevens emigrated out to Australia in 1950 aboard the *Mooltan*. She later recalled,

Many of us did not want to leave Britain, our homeland, but the country was pretty shabby after the war and well into the 1950s. There was still bomb damage around by the time of the Coronation in June 1953. There were still power blackouts and many lights, even in hotels, were turned off during daytime. There was no money and far too few jobs. Families were often crammed together in tiny houses with little comfort and even less privacy. These houses were often freezing cold in winter. Myself, I well remember the winter of 1947 – it was one of the worst in anyone's memory – and there was too little coal for heating. Even trains stopped and the country came to a standstill. New, prefabricated bungalows were created after the war and cost less than £1,000, but these were often poorly constructed with leaky roofs and inferior fittings. Rationing continued as well, of course, and often seemed worse than in the war years. Everything it seemed – from clothes to sugar to meats – remained on strict ration. Many people felt the strain. The future and our own future did not look bright. So, Britain was not a pleasant or even happy place then. Australia seemed, in contrast, like a faraway paradise and which was plentiful, promising and happy. We saw posters, colorful, bright and showing sunshine – even modern cities and idyllic beaches. And so, my family sailed off from London, aboard that old P&O liner, and said goodbye. We did not return for over fifteen years, until a trip in the *Oriana* in the late 1960s.

Living in Melbourne for over sixty years, Frank Bucklow emigrated on P&O as well and added,

Australia was almost desperate for skilled people – doctors, dentists, nurses and teachers – in the late 1940s and 1950s. They wanted architects and designers, skilled factory workers and even farmers as well. The £10 assisted fare plan was created for that reason. It was £10 for adults, £5 for teenagers and children went free. It was a popular program that attracted great numbers of people. Australia also welcomed newcomers, especially from Britain, to build up and even strengthen its population in the western part of the country. Western Australia was very nearly invaded by the Japanese during the Second World War and there was concern about its future even into the 1950s.

There were 240,000 applicants soon after the £10 program started, in May 1947; this had jumped to 400,000 by November. At the same time, 5,000 were employed just in making the Resettlement Scheme work. Posters were displayed through Britain – Australia was the promised land! Companies such as P&O and the Orient Line had a guaranteed, post-war market – older ships could be all tourist class, primarily carrying these new settlers; new liners could quickly fill all of their tourist-class quarters.

Old-timers like *Mooltan* and *Maloja* soldiered on, until 1953–54, when the likes of the brand-new, much improved *Arcadia* and *Iberia* first appeared. The two earlier ships, by then past thirty, went to the scrappers – the *Mooltan* ended her days at Faslane and the *Maloja* at Inverkeithing. Both ships left impressive records – each had completed eighty round trips to Australia.

The veteran *Mooltan* on her way to the breakers at Faslane. (P&O)

3

CHITRAL AND *RANCHI*

In 1925, P&O built a trio of 15,500-ton sisters – the *Cathay*, *Comorin* and *Chitral*. Only the *Chitral* survived the war, however, and was recommissioned: 'Pressed into much needed service,' said Captain Philip Jackson, 'and primarily for migrant sailings to Australia, in 1948.' A 548-foot-long ship, she had been built by Alexander Stephen & Sons on the Clyde, at Glasgow. She and her two sisters were used on the London–Australia run until 1933 when they were switched to Indian service as well as sailings out to the Far East, to Singapore, Shanghai, Hong Kong, Kobe and Yokohama.

Used as an armed merchant cruiser during the early years of the Second World War, the *Chitral* was rebuilt at Baltimore in 1944 as a troopship. She served in this role until released, and returned to P&O in September 1947.

The *Chitral* was restored, with 738 total berths, accommodated in some two- and four-berth cabins, but mostly eight- and ten-berth migrant quarters. Although a comparatively austere ship after the war, she had a prized amenity for the long, often very hot migrant sailings to and from Australia – two outdoor swimming pools.

A regular on the Australian migrant run, she carried regular passengers on the return voyages and, on occasion, called at Indonesian ports to collect Dutch nationals returning home following independence. The 16-knot *Chitral* endured until she was retired and scrapped at Dalmuir in Scotland in April 1953.

In 1925, P&O also built four 17,000-ton liners purposely for its London–Bombay service. They were dubbed the 'R Class' and named *Ranpura*, *Ranchi*, *Rawalpindi* and *Rajputana*. They were rather interesting-looking twin-stackers, designed for 308 first-class and 282 second-class passengers. The *Ranchi* survived the war, however, and then she too was restored but for migrant service. The twin-funnel ship was constructed by Hawthorn Leslie & Co. at Newcastle, but was refitted after the war with only one funnel. In her post-war mode, the *Ranchi* was very austere, very basic – with her passengers only in eight-, ten- and twelve-berth cabins. She was growing old, tired and troubled, according to the late Peter Dawson, a P&O steward: 'She was very tender in her advancing years.' On one return voyage, she broke down in the Suez Canal and blocked eighty ships before being towed away for repairs. Her end came in December 1952; she was delivered to shipbreakers at Newport in Monmouthshire a month later.

By 1948, P&O was operating four purposeful migrant ships to Australia – *Maloja*, *Mooltan*, *Chitral* and *Ranchi*. Often, these ships – serving in the twilight of their careers – were booked to capacity on their homeward sailings; they returned with budget tourists.

The migrant trade to Australia flourished, such that P&O considered building a special liner, a 30,000-tonner created by Harland & Wolff at Belfast, for as many as 3,000 migrants and low-fare passengers. Later refined to 2,300 passengers, such a ship, it was planned, would be introduced at the end of 1949. Said to cost over £3½ million, the high cost was the final blow and the project never materialized. Then there was a further plan, based on the estimate that there might be as many as 75,000 migrants per year going out to Australia, to build four or five migrant liners that could make four sailings each per year. This was abandoned in favor of another short-lived scheme – converting aircraft carriers, with their vast internal spaces, to migrant carriers. HMS *Victorious*, an Invincible class carrier completed in 1941, was actually seriously considered, carrying 1,000 passengers and being manned on the UK–Australia service by the Royal Australian Navy. Finally, there was the HMS *Majestic*, a carrier launched in February 1945, too late for war service, and laid up. The plan in 1947 was to refit her to carry 2,000 migrants. Further studies, however, prompted concerns about the ship's stability with passengers aboard and also even the most basic comforts for her travelers. This plan was dropped as well and instead, quite coincidentally, the unfinished carrier was purchased by the Australian navy in 1949, renamed HMAS *Melbourne* and finally commissioned in the summer of 1955. She served as Australia's naval flagship for the next twenty-six years.

The need for low-fare berths was further expanded in 1947 by the needs of the IRO, the International Refugee Organization, for thousands of displaced peoples (often from northern Europe, mostly from the Baltic states) to be transported to Australia and elsewhere. These people were existing in the most basic of conditions, usually in internment camps that were of a lower standard than any British migrant ship. The combination of the British-Australian resettlement program and the IRO would mean 170,000 passengers – or possibly as many as 200,000 – over a six-year period, until 1953–54. Unquestionably, more and preferably bigger ships were needed. Even combination passenger-cargo ships such as the 11,100-grt *Port Hobart* of the Port Line was put to use – she was refitted to carry up to 130 migrants per voyage. The British Government converted the fire-gutted liner *Monarch of Bermuda*, built in 1931 for luxury cruising, to the 1,600-berth migrant ship *New Australia*. She was added to UK–Australia service in 1950. Many other liners, some quite aged, were pressed into low-fare service as well.

Busy voyages. The post-war *Chitral* was used on the very busy Australian migrant run. (P&O)

After service in the Second World War, the *Ranchi* was refitted with one instead of her original two funnels. (Alex Duncan)

4

ORONTES

Britain's Orient Line was well-known until the 1960s as a great passenger ship company. They were known for their large, very comfortable and often innovative liners that ran on the then busy sea route between Britain and Australia, which used the customary routing through the Mediterranean, the Suez Canal, the Red Sea and then across the Indian Ocean. A more exact routing was from London to Gibraltar, Naples, Piraeus, Port Said, Aden, Colombo and then over to Fremantle, Melbourne and Sydney. London–Sydney took twenty-eight to thirty-five days in those pre-jet times, even well into the 1960s, and cost $400 in first class and $200 in the more austere, lower-deck tourist class.

After suffering some losses during the Second World War, the London-headquartered Orient Line, a firm actually controlled by its greatest rival, the P&O Line, revived several older passenger ships so as to resume their busy Australian liner service. There were businessmen, government officials and the odd tourist in first class, and thousands of immigrants wanting to leave a war-weary, still rationed Britain for better lives in the land 'Down Under' in tourist class. The alternatives for migrants were the USA, Canada and South and East Africa.

Tony Ralph, a very keen ocean liner enthusiast who lived in Sydney in the 1960s and who later became tour manager aboard Cunard's *Queen Elizabeth 2*, recalled one of these older Orient Line passenger ships, the 20,000-grt *Orontes*: 'She and the *Orion* [built in 1935] were two of my favorites from my ship-watching days back then,' he said. 'They were glimpses of pre-war, of an almost bygone age. I could look back to the 1920s and 1930s, but in the early 1960s. Orient Line was considered by many Australians to be the finest company on the UK–Suez–Australia trade and their ships were special.'

The Orient Line made a huge investment in the UK–Australia trade between 1924 and 1929 by building no less than five new, 20,000-grt liners. They were the *Orama* (1924), *Oronsay* and *Otranto* (1925), *Orford* (1928) and *Orontes* (1929). Built by Vickers-Armstrong Limited at Barrow-in-Furness, these twin-stackers had accommodations for nearly 1,700 passengers each – 572 in first class and 1,114 in third class (the latter improved and reduced to 500 tourist class by 1933). Used mostly on the UK–Australia run, they also went cruising, to Scandinavia, the Mediterranean and the Atlantic isles mostly, with a much-reduced capacity of 550 passengers in an all-first-class configuration.

With her twin, pencil-thin stacks, the *Orontes* was all but a curiosity to Tony Ralph: 'She still had her original black hull whereas all the other Orient Line passenger ships had rather unique corn-colored hulls,' he recalled.

By the early 1960s, the *Orontes* was the eldest in the then combined P&O-Orient fleet and was used as an all-one-class, all-migrant ship. Most other P&O-Orient liners were still two class. I saw the *Orontes* arrive with over a thousand migrants aboard and with thousands of relatives and well-wishers waiting on the quayside. Often, little English was spoken among the passengers. There were lots of southern Italians and southern Greeks onboard. They were not your typical Italians and Greeks – they were farmers, workers, very basic people. They'd never traveled before, never been aboard a ship and many had never even seen the ocean. The ship itself smelled of garlic and exotic foods. It was the flavors and smells of another world to us, to insular Australians. Ships like the *Orontes* with her all-migrant passengers were unique.

Captain Bob Ellingham recalled a near-disaster aboard the *Orontes* in 1961. The ship was then very close to the end of her days.

We were at Marseilles and swept from the breakwater to the dock by 100 mph winds from the notorious *Mistral*. We dragged the tugs as well as our own anchors. We rammed the dock, finishing with a big hole in the stern. Fortunately, there were no casualties. We were on a homeward voyage from Australia. We kept the passengers on for the night and then sent them by train to London. Temporary repairs were made, after which we took the empty *Orontes* home to England for a thorough patching. Ironically, I met my future wife on that trip.

A year later, in March 1962, Captain Ellingham was among the fifty-odd crew that took the thirty-three-year-old *Orontes* out to the scrappers at Valencia in Spain. She was to have been sold to Italian breakers at La Spezia, but the deal fell through and instead she went for over £232,000 to the Spanish.

We crept along, taking sixteen days from the Tilbury Docks. At sea, we were advised that we could have any keepsakes we wished. With no time for shipping arrangements from Spain, this was rather disappointing as the ship was fully fitted: bedding, linen, silverware, furniture and even the old grand piano.

The classic-looking *Orontes* departing Sydney on another homeward voyage to the UK. (Lindsay Johnson Collection)

Loading migrants. The *Orontes* seen at Naples on an outward voyage to Australia. (Richard Weiss Collection)

5

OTRANTO

A senior P&O-Orient assistant purser had great regard for company passenger ships and named her home Otranto House. The 20,000-grt liner, first commissioned in 1925, was nearly a casualty a year later. While on a Mediterranean cruise, she hit the rocks at Cape Matapan and subsequently had serious bow damages. She needed lengthy repairs afterward. The 659-foot-long *Otranto* went on to do yeoman duty during the Second World War – serving as a troopship, then as a landing ship and finally reverting to trooping.

Refitted by Cammell Laird of Birkenhead after the war, she was restyled for the migrant trade – carrying up to 1,416 all-tourist-class passengers. She resumed Australian service in July 1949 and completed sixty-four round trips to Australia before her end came. Old age turned against her in early 1957 when she began suffering from engine troubles. There was little reluctance in letting her go after thirty-two years. That June, she was handed over to breakers at Faslane.

Traditional design. The *Otranto* departing Sydney. (Lindsay Johnson Collection)

Chance meeting. The *Otranto* and *Orontes* seen together at Hobart in 1955. (P&O)

6

STRATHNAVER AND *STRATHAIRD*

P&O certainly built some beautiful, very interesting passenger ships in its long, colorful history of over 175 years. Among the most exciting ships were the famed Strath liners of the 1930s. The first two of five were the sisters *Strathaird* and *Strathnaver*.

Previously, up until the late 1920s, P&O passenger ships – with such appropriate sounding names for Eastern services as *Rawalpindi*, *Viceroy of India*, *Cathay* and *Bendigo* – were mostly conservative vessels, all reflections of conservative British design and quiet British taste. It was not until the early thirties that the company, wanting to strengthen its competitive edge against such rivals as the Orient Line and Shaw Savill, embarked on a plan of new-style passenger liners. These became the biggest, finest and fastest P&O liners yet. The Strath naming was derived from Lord Inchcape of Strathnaver, a long-serving P&O chairman.

The first of these new ships were delivered by Vickers-Armstrong in 1931–32. At over 22,500 tons, the *Strathaird* and *Strathnaver* were very contemporary ships and offered a new level of comfort for the Australian run that included every passenger cabin having running water. They were also designed with a provision for cruising, mostly of a two- or three-week duration, from London or Southampton to the Atlantic isles, the Mediterranean, the northern cities and the Norwegian fjords, and at a later time, from Sydney to the South Pacific islands. In December 1932, the 664-foot-long *Strathaird* made the very first P&O cruise from Australia – a five-night cruise

from Sydney to Norfolk Island and back. As expected, these twins – dubbed 'the White Ships' – were a huge success.

Each of that first pair of sisters had three funnels, a design element used to remind travelers on routes east of Suez of the big Atlantic liners. The two ships also introduced the all-white hull coloring at P&O for a cooler, more tropical look. Previously, P&O was noted for using dark colors, including an all-black hull and upper works.

So successful was this first pair that P&O, even while coping with the difficulties of the worldwide Depression, opted to build a successor, the 22,000-grt, single-stack *Strathmore*, in 1935, and then the twin sisters *Stratheden* and *Strathallan* in 1937–38. Divided into two classes for some 1,200 passengers, the *Strathaird* and *Strathnaver* were splendid ships in every way. These Strath liners were the pride of the P&O fleet up until the Second World War and were among the most popular liners in the UK–Australia trade.

All were restored in the late 1940s, following Allied trooping duties, except for the *Strathallan*, which was torpedoed and sunk in 1942. The refitted *Strathaird* returned to commercial service in January 1948; the *Strathnaver* resumed commercial service, following long, much extended wartime and then post-war military service, in January 1950. Her refit took over a year, complicated by troubles at British shipyards: too many ships and too little space at overcrowded national shipyards, a shortage of materials, sky-rocketing conversion costs, and labor unrest, as well as strikes. In 1954, replacing the *Mooltan* and *Maloja* primarily in the booming migrant trade, this pair was converted to all tourist class. The year before, in June 1953, the *Strathnaver* had represented P&O at the Coronation Fleet Review for Queen Elizabeth II.

After serving on several P&O cargo ships, Philip Jackson transferred, in the early 1950s, to some of the famed P&O passenger liners. 'The Company procedure was then fairly well established,' he recalled.

A third mate's position on a freighter led to a third mate's role on a passenger ship. My first assignments were on the earliest of our Strath liners, the *Strathnaver* and *Strathaird*. They were then still two-class ships. Passengers in first class seemed to all but rattle around in very spacious quarters. There were mostly service and commercial people, the equivalent of today's airline first and club classes. In the tourist section, we had mostly migrants, who were traveling under a special fare of £10. The Australian government wanted to increase its population and especially to expand its competitive technological force. These low fares were outward resettlement passages. Homebound, we would carry many Australian families, many of whom would be on three- to six-month cultural and family visits to Britain and around Continental Europe.

In the 1950s, the four Strath liners (the others being the *Strathmore* and *Stratheden*) worked a balanced schedule between London, Gibraltar, Aden, Bombay, Colombo, Adelaide, Fremantle, Melbourne and Sydney. Philip Jackson, later Captain Jackson, added,

We had 2½ weeks at the Tilbury Docks in London for unloading and then loading of cargo, which was very much a part of our liner operation. For the passengers, tugs would later move these liners to the Tilbury Landing Stage for four–five hours, and to meet the special 'boat trains' that were up from Fenchurch Street station in London. Of course, physically, our liners differed from the rest of the fleet in that they had white hulls and yellow funnels. The freighters had black hulls and black funnels. The passengers were made to appear lighter and more tropical looking, were easier to maintain and were, in fact, as much as 10° cooler on the inside. There was very limited air conditioning, if any at all, on the Straths or any other P&O liners until the late 1950s.

'They were lovely, very traditional ships,' recalled Tony Ralph, a keen observer of passenger ships in Sydney harbor during the 1960s.

They had very stately, very English interiors. They were classic British ocean liners to Australians. By the early 1960s, the older *Strathaird* and *Strathnaver* had long been made over as all one class and catered to the low-fare migrant trade from London via Suez to Fremantle, Melbourne and Sydney. They carried budget Australian tourists bound for British and European visits on their return trips.

These sisters finished their days out in Hong Kong – the *Strathaird* arrived at local shipbreakers there in July 1961, the *Strathnaver* in April 1962.

Above left: Tearful day. The *Strathnaver* leaving Sydney for the very last time in 1962. (Lindsay Johnson Collection)

Above: Splendor at sea. The first-class main lounge aboard the *Strathaird*. (P&O)

Left: After dinner. The Smoking Room on B Deck aboard the *Strathaird*. (P&O)

Traveling across the Empire! A poster noting the easily connecting services of P&O and the British India Line. (P&O)

A poster from the 1930s showing the homeward journey to England on the beautiful Strath liners. (P&O)

7

CORFU AND CARTHAGE

'They were, in ways, rather plain ships – designed for a specific purpose and trade, and without the frills,' noted Captain Philip Jackson. 'I often saw them berthed in the London Docks on their two-week layovers between long voyages out to the Far East and back.' Originally intended to be the *Chefoo* and *Canton*, this pair was named *Corfu* and *Carthage* and delivered two months apart, in September and November 1931. Built at Glasgow, these 14,200-tonners had two funnels and black hulls. Used as armed merchant cruisers and then transports during the war years, they were refitted and rebuilt with single stacks and all-white hulls in the late 1940s. They resumed sailing out to Singapore, Penang and Hong Kong, carrying 181 passengers in first class and 213 in tourist class. First class had all single or double cabins, eight of which had private bathroom facilities. The deluxe cabins were air conditioned in 1959. Teamed with the larger, newer *Chusan* and the similar *Canton*, they were retired in 1961 and sold to Japanese shipbreakers – the *Corfu* was broken up at Niihama, the *Carthage* at Osaka.

The *Corfu* at Cape Town. (Steffen Weirauch Collection)

The *Corfu* in wartime dress, departing from Southampton with 2,200 military passengers aboard. (Cronican-Arroyo Collection)

8

ORION

Tony Ralph remembered the *Orion* from her visits to Sydney:

The *Orion* had exceptional art deco interiors, styling that made her more like one of the famed transatlantic liners than one on the Australian run. She was also a pioneer of sorts for the Orient Line. She made the first trip, in 1954, of an expanded Orient Line service over to New Zealand and then up to Hawaii and the North American West Coast. Orient was looking for more passengers by then, to expand, to offer an almost worldwide service. Hereafter, you could take a liner such as the 1,400-passenger *Orion* up to Vancouver or San Francisco or Los Angeles.

Captain Bob Ellingham recalled this expanded service:

In the mid-fifties, the P&O and Orient lines began to spread their range across the Pacific to North America and thereby becoming the most diverse liner operation in the world. However, this initial expansion was not without its problems. I can remember steaming into San Francisco in the old *Orion* with ten first-class passengers aboard. We simply weren't known in America and the few who had heard of us thought we were a Japanese company.

Commissioned in August 1935, the 23,600-grt *Orion* was an innovative, very significant liner constructed by Vickers-Armstrong at Barrow-in-Furness. A sister, the *Orcades*, completed in 1937, became a war loss, being torpedoed and sunk in October 1942. The 665-foot-long *Orion* had been named by the Duke of Gloucester, third son of King George V and Queen Mary, but he was in faraway Brisbane on launching day (7 December 1934). A radio signal was sent by the duke to the shipyard, which in turn released the liner from the slipway and started her launch. Perhaps even more significantly, she was the first Orient liner with one funnel, the first with one mast and the first with a corn-colored hull. Her interior design – introducing softer colors and sleek styling – was the start of high art deco on the Australian run. She reminded many of the great, distantly well-known Atlantic liners. She had extra amenities as well that included air conditioning in both her first- and tourist-class dining rooms, a novelty for the 1930s. She was in fact the very first British liner with air conditioning. Returning to service in February 1947 after valiant services in the Second World War as a trooper, her refurbishment cost £500,000, and her passenger configuration was restyled for 550 in first class and 700 in tourist class. These numbers changed during a refit in 1958, becoming 342 cabin class and 722 tourist. There was another change, in 1960, this time to 1,691 all-one-class passengers.

In 1963, David Carr – then a young junior officer – was assigned to the veteran *Orion*, by then the oldest liner in the P&O-Orient fleet. She was, however, nearing her end. 'I was aboard her final sailings out to Australia,' he recalled years later, in November 1983, during a cruise aboard the *Cunard Countess*. By then, he was a chief officer with Cunard.

After sailing from London, we put into Piraeus in Greece to load a large group of Greek immigrants. Homeward, we returned with some disgruntled immigrants, who disliked Australia and Australian life, and lots of young Australian girls, who were headed for tours of Europe or temporary jobs in Britain. With very limited air conditioning, the *Orion* was among the last P&O liners without the amenity of fully air-conditioned quarters. I can recall the captain sometimes turning the ship around for ten minutes or so just to catch a Red Sea breeze.

In the end, in May 1963, rather than going direct to the scrapheap, the *Orion* was chartered for several months to serve as a floating hotel at Hamburg for the International Gardening Exhibition, accommodating up to 1,150 guests. Prior to her arrival at the German port, special preparations were made for her to berth at the Overseas Landing Stage. David Carr recalled, 'As we arrived, the pre-constructed, special walkways to the ship were mismeasured and did not fit. They had to be redone.'

With her duties finished, the twenty-eight-year-old *Orion* left Hamburg on 1 October 1963 for Tamise in nearby Belgium, where she was broken up.

Above: Wartime coloring. The *Orion* arrives at Fremantle at the end of the Second World War, in 1945. (P&O)

Right: A great Orient Line favorite. The art-deco-styled *Orion* seen at Hobart on 10 October 1957. (P&O)

CRUISES from AUSTRALIA

WINTER, 1938

FIJI - PAPUA* - NOUMEA*

*Via Great Barrier Reef.

No. 34. June 3 to 16 . . . FIJI   †"ORONSAY," 20,000 tons
No. 35. July 1 to 14 . . . PAPUA   ‡"ORONTES," 20,000 tons
No. 36. July 29 to Aug. 11 NOUMEA   †"ORAMA,"   20,000 tons
No. 37. Aug. 26 to Sept. 8 FIJI   †"OTRANTO," 20,000 tons

†First Saloon from 20 gns. and Tourist B from 12 gns.
‡First Saloon from 20 gns. and Tourist from 13 gns.

Inside the limits of the usual annual vacation, Orient Line Winter Cruises will bring within your reach pleasant tropic islands in the romantic South Seas . . . . And as you travel you will enjoy the advantages of Orient Line comfort, service and cuisine.

An Orient Line Cruise is very easy to arrange—and very easy, indeed, to enjoy.

The earlier you book, the wider is your choice of cabins

Orient Steam Navigation Co. Ltd., Incorporated in England

J.S. PTY. LTD.

Early cruising. Orient Line cruises from Australia for the winter of 1938. (P&O)

Interior Perspective

ORIENT LINE
R-M-STEAMER
"ORCADES"

The cover of a 1937 booklet heralding the innovative decorative stylings of the *Orcades* and her sister *Orion*. (P&O)

Aboard *Orion*. The first-class dining room with looking glass by E. McKnight Kauffer. (P&O)

Classic 1930s style. The first-class main lounge aboard the 1935-built *Orion*. (P&O)

9

STRATHMORE

'Among the four post-war Strath liners, the slightly larger *Strathmore* and *Stratheden* were the better ships, remained two class and also did some cruises from Sydney,' recalled Tony Ralph. 'They sailed on holiday trips over to New Zealand and to the South Pacific islands, and offered bargain fares to Australian vacationers.'

The 23,500-grt *Strathmore*, named at launching at Barrow by the Duchess of York, later Queen Elizabeth and later still the Queen Mother, was delivered in September 1935. The duchess's father was the Earl of Strathmore. She was the third Strath liner, but slightly larger, improved, somewhat more comfortable and with a design change: she had only a single funnel atop her all-white hull.

The 20-knot *Strathmore* had a long wartime career, from September 1939 until the summer of 1948. She resumed London–Australia sailings in October 1949, by then with a more contemporary balance of 497 first-class and 487 tourist-class passengers.

The 665-foot-long *Strathmore* as well as the *Stratheden* also made some cruises from Britain in the early 1960s. The late Frank Jackson and his wife Evelyn acted as combined port lecturer and shore excursions manager. He remembered,

There were occasional cruises on the *Strathmore* and *Stratheden* in the 1950s and early 1960s, usually fourteen days from London to the Mediterranean or to the Canary Islands, Madeira, Spain and Portugal. These were scheduled between regular Australian line voyages. They were actually old-fashioned ships by then, but very gracious. We actually had many well-to-do passengers on these cruises, many of them well educated and wanting greater cultural enrichment from their trip. They liked the experience of visiting other lands, seeing other peoples. They were not especially interested in the likes of magicians and cabaret. Onboard, the only formal entertainment was the orchestra. There was no cruise director then. Activities were organized by the purser's department and the passengers.

Restyled in 1954 (like the very similar *Stratheden*) for the migrant and low-fare tourist trades, the two liners became one-class ships with 1,200 berths each. However, as the migrant trade slowly declined in the early sixties, the aging Strath liners were made redundant. While the older *Strathnaver* and *Strathaird* sailed off to the breakers in 1961–62, the *Strathmore* was retired in the summer of 1963. She was laid up for months and might well have gone to the breakers as well, but then was sold to Greek buyers, the Latsis Line, owned by billionaire oil and tanker tycoon John S. Latsis. Delivered at Piraeus that November, the *Strathmore* was promptly renamed *Marianna Latsi* and then used, but only for part of the year, carrying religious pilgrims to and from Jeddah. Most voyages began in North and West African ports. For the remainder of the year, she and her near-sister, *Henrietta Latsi* (ex-*Stratheden*), were laid up. In 1966, for unknown reasons, the two ships swapped names – the *Marianna Latsi* (ex-*Strathmore*) became the *Henrietta Latsi*; the *Henrietta Latsi* (ex-*Stratheden*) changed to *Marianna Latsi*. The end was not far off, however.

In 1969, both ships were sold to Italian shipbreakers and were demolished almost side by side at La Spezia.

Handsome good looks! The fine-looking *Strathmore*, completed in 1935. (P&O)

10

STRATHEDEN

'I have only done two cruises, but fifty years apart,' shared Nula Bryant. We met onboard the *Adonia* during a twenty-one-night cruise to the Mediterranean in July 2012. That voyage was part of P&O's gala 175th anniversary celebrations, and included the simultaneous departure of seven P&O cruise ships from Southampton. It was the grandest ever procession of liners in peacetime. It was Nula's second P&O voyage. The first was aboard another P&O liner, the *Stratheden*, back in 1962 on a three-week cruise from Southampton to the Mediterranean. She recalled,

> It was a great adventure for my sister and myself. The ship seemed absolutely huge and like a hotel, the food servings were enormous and there was ice cream handed out every afternoon from a man carrying a frozen box. But to two teenage girls, the very best fun was riding the ship's elevators. The elevator boys wore red uniforms, looked so smart and, being slightly older, we were deeply attracted. And I remember that they were quite good-looking as well.

Commissioned in December 1937, the design and decoration of the 23,400-grt *Stratheden* was influenced very much by the innovative *Orion*, completed two years before but for the Orient Line. Both liners were of very similar dimensions, and were constructed by Vickers Armstrong at Barrow. Her sister, the *Strathallan*, delivered to P&O in March 1938, was a war loss, being torpedoed in the Mediterranean in December 1942. Once

the fifth ship was delivered, it completed what many considered P&O's most successful team of ships, 'the Straths'. They became familiar, highly recognizable sights in the London Docks, at Tilbury and Southampton, passing through the Mediterranean and Suez, steaming across the Indian Ocean and along the waterfronts of far-off Fremantle, Melbourne and Sydney. 'Along with the decoratively innovative *Orion* and *Orcades*, the Straths were very popular and highly distinctive in Australia,' recalled the late Frank Andrews, a ship-watching Melbourne native of the 1920s and 1930s. 'It was always rather special when one of these big liners were in port. Just before the war started, they were the biggest liners in regular Australian service.'

The *Stratheden*, serving as a troopship for over six years (steaming over 468,000 miles and carrying just under 150,000 troops), was called to war while on a return sailing from Australia in September 1939. Her officers and crew were later recognized for their brave efforts during the final days of that twenty-eight-night voyage from Sydney. The *Stratheden* was the first ship to pass through the enemy's submarine zone of the Mediterranean and eastern Atlantic after war had been declared (on 3 September).

The 664-foot-long *Stratheden* took part in the Allied invasion of North Africa, where her sister, the *Strathallan*, had been sunk. She later made a transatlantic crossing to Quebec City. Her engines stood up exceptionally well to the severe demands of war service, during which the 20-knot, twin-screw ship never missed a sailing – a tribute to both her builders and her engine room staff.

The handsome *Stratheden* was reconditioned and returned to P&O's London–Australia service in June 1947. Her accommodations were arranged for 527 first class and 453 tourist class, of which a lower grade, referred to as 'Tourist B' class, was especially for post-war migrants. Her post-war accommodation was nearly identical to its initial standard. The original paneling and glass murals in the public rooms were not stripped during the war, but instead boarded up. Excellent use was made of Australian walnut, elm burr, sycamore, betula and other Empire woods, and the lighting and furniture were said to combine comfort with restraint. There was a particularly inviting swimming pool, especially useful on her long, warm-weather voyages to and from Australia. The appointments in the less expensive tourist class were said to fall little, if at all, short of first class. A post-war innovation, later extended to other P&O liners, was the presence of two lady stenographers, ranking as junior officers in the purser's department, and four telephonists, mostly recruited from the WRNS.

In 1950, the *Stratheden* made an unusual detour for a P&O liner in peacetime – she made four charter voyages for Cunard between Southampton and New York. On 16 June, *The New York Times* reported,

A British luxury liner with a largely Oriental crew emerged from the fog-shrouded entrance to New York harbor early yesterday morning and steamed virtually unnoticed to a North River pier. She is the *Stratheden*, completing her maiden voyage to this port as a passenger liner. Inbound from Southampton and Le Havre with 450 passengers, the all-white vessel was finally warped into a position alongside Pier 90, at West 50th Street, at 8.00 a.m. Though no welcome, official or otherwise, awaited her, she was one of the most colorful ships to enter the port since the war. As longshoremen raised the gangway, Ebrahim Mohamed, chief *serang* – boatswain – of the liner appeared in Indian costume, with red and silver turban, and blew a sharp blast on a small silver whistle. The signal brought immediate action. Several Lascar deckhands, in similar attire, scurried to secure the gangway and then stood at attention with arms crossed as passengers filed off the ship.

'There were sixty-three of these men aboard,' added the *Times* report.

All are Moslem recruited by Ebrahim Mohamed in Kathiawar, India. Despite the present discord between India and Pakistan, they share quarters with 50 Pakistani Moslems employed in the engine department and 148 natives from Portugese Goa. The Goans are all Roman Catholics and served in the catering department.

The thirty-eight-year-old *serang* said through an interpreter that he went to sea at the age of ten as a 'punkah boy' for P&O. He added that he was following a career similar to that of his father and grandfather, who served as chief *serangs* in their day. 'I love the sea,' he said, 'and I am no stranger to New York.' He explained that he had come here several times on troopships and served for a time on the French *Île de France* during the war, a ship managed by P&O in the early 1940s.

The 261 Asiatics make up nearly half of the *Stratheden*'s crew. According to Chief Steward Arthur Cookson, they get along 'famously' with the British personnel. A tour of the crew quarters, led by Mr Cookson, unfolded a picturesque scene. In the quarters of the Goans was a large altar on which was placed a picture of Pope Pius XII. One crewmember had just lit a candle and was kneeling in prayer. Fifty feet beyond, off a narrow passageway, was the Moslem prayer room. Originally intended as a mess hall, it was converted to a religious center by crewmen who resigned themselves to eating their own meals in their various bunks. The room was immaculately clean and contained a dozen or more prayer rugs. Hoossein Fackeer, leader of the Pakistani Moslems, explained that the faithful come to the room five times a day to pray. Shoes are left outside in the corridor, he said. His flowing mustache and closely cropped hair apparently had been dyed red. Asked why, he replied, 'This is my privilege, for I have been to Mecca.'

After returning to the Australian run, the *Stratheden* made further news in March 1955. It was reported,

The tiny Greek freighter *Iason* foundered in a storm off the toe of Italy and nineteen men perished during the rescue operation. Eleven members of the *Iason*'s crew and eight members of a small boat crew from the British liner *Stratheden* drowned when crashing seas capsized the lifeboat. Four members of the *Iason*'s crew were saved, including the captain and first mate. The *Stratheden*, bound from Australia to Great Britain, went to the help of the *Iason*, a 449-ton converted corvette, after receiving distress calls from the Ionian Sea. The *Iason* was heading home from Sicily. She had disappeared when the *Stratheden* reached the scene and the crew was struggling in the water.

It was decided that these last of the Strath liners would be retired from P&O-Orient service in the summer of 1963. On 19 June, *The Shipping World* carried a story especially about the aging *Stratheden*:

The P&O liner *Stratheden* is to be withdrawn from regular Australian mail service when she returns from her voyage terminating at London on 23 October. Following this, the ship has been chartered to Mr Max Wilson as an additional cruise ship for his Travel Savings Association, the TSA, for a series of four winter cruises between December 1963 and March 1964. The P&O Company will provide the ship and ship's company and normal tourist one-class service. Berthing, booking, itineraries, shore excursions and entertainments onboard are the responsibilities of the charterers. The future of the *Stratheden* after the charter has not yet been decided.

The Shipping World continued,

The success of the Travel Savings cruise program has been such that a change in plans has proved necessary. Three of the 20 cruises on the *Empress of Britain* from the UK are being replaced by the *Stratheden*'s cruises to allow the former ship to join the *Empress of England* in South Africa during December 1963 and January 1964. The cruises to be operated by the *Stratheden* are: 2nd December, London–Casablanca–Gibraltar–Lisbon–London, with fares from 18 pounds from TSA members; 11th December, a similar cruise, but from Southampton; 20th December, Southampton–Madeira–Tenerife–Las Palmas–Ceuta–Lisbon–Southampton; and on 4th January, Southampton–Las Palmas–Trinidad–Curaçao–Jamaica–Barbados–Madeira–Southampton.

'Travel Savings is reported to be interested in actually purchasing a ship,' the article further reported,

and at present are attempting to obtain the Portuguese liner *Vera Cruz*, which is being sold by the Companhia Colonial de

Navegação. There are reported to be three parties interested in the ship, two Greek owners, John S. Latsis and A. J. Chandris, the latter of which is urgently requiring a replacement vessel for the *Brittany* recently lost by fire, and, of course, the TSA. Owing to the competition, the price is reported to have been considerably forced up to about 3,000,000 pounds.

The *Stratheden*, along with the *Strathmore*, was, in fact, sold to John S. Latsis. The *Strathmore* was delivered at Piraeus in November 1963 and became the *Marianna Latsi* (although she was initially thought to be named *Marianna II*) while the *Stratheden* was delivered in March 1964 and changed to *Henrietta Latsi*. The *Marianna Latsi* was used during the early part of 1964 and 1965 to make a few pilgrim voyages between Libya and Jeddah; the *Henrietta Latsi* began in winter 1965, from both North and West African ports to Jeddah. Thereafter, the ships were used between March and May, but then sat idle for the rest of the year. In 1966, for some unexplained reason, their names were switched – the *Marianna Latsi* became the *Henrietta Latsi* and vice versa. The question of names actually became more confusing after the launch in Japan, in February 1966, of a 45,000-grt tanker named *Henrietta Latsi*.

Both laid up in Greek backwaters in their very final years, they were sold, in May 1969, to Italian scrap merchants and broken up at La Spezia. Both ships had given long service and were over thirty years of age.

Above: Another beautiful-looking ship, the *Stratheden*, passing under the Sydney Harbour Bridge. (P&O)

Right: A postcard highlighting the interiors of the *Stratheden*. (P&O)

11

EMPIRE ORWELL

The author almost visited the former *Empire Orwell* in the summer of 1984. Nearly fifty years of age, she was historic in passenger ship circles of the time. We were visiting Djakarta on a cruise from Singapore, sailing aboard the chartered West German cruise ship *Princess Mahsuri* (ex-*Berlin*). I'd mentioned to the captain that she had been a German passenger liner from the 1930s and, of course, he too then became keenly interested. He radioed ahead to the port agents and asked to arrange a visit. She was by then in military service and so the arrangements were somewhat complicated, tangled in red tape even. Eventually, it was approved. But then the chance vanished. Although the ship was moored in Djakarta harbor for two years, she had just sailed, almost the very day before our arrival, on a military assignment. It was indeed disappointing.

The 577-foot-long ship was indeed very interesting and quite historic. By 1984, she was nearly fifty years old. Built by Blohm & Voss, the illustrious Hamburg-based shipbuilders, she and a twin sister were constructed for the German East Africa Line and its service from Hamburg to West, South and East African ports. Named *Pretoria* (her sister was the *Windhuk*), these 16,600-grt ships were sturdy-looking twin-stackers, carrying lots of cargo but a rather scant number of passengers, 490 in all (and in two classes). Her maiden voyage had added drama – she went aground in the Solent near Southampton on Christmas Eve 1936. Five tugs attempted to free her but failed. Some 900 tons of water were discharged and then 400 tons of fuel oil transferred to a small tanker before seven tugs finally succeeded. Six months later, there was more drama for the *Pretoria*. She collided with a British tanker, the *Hekla*, in thick fog in the North Sea. The tanker was badly damaged.

Used during the Second World War by the Nazi regime as an accommodation center (at Kiel, Neustadt, Hamburg and then Pillau) and then a hospital ship, the 18-knot ship was called to sea duties in the winter of 1945 to help with the evacuation of the Nazi Eastern Territories. She survived, but only to become a prize of war, at Copenhagen, for the invading British forces. First renamed *Empire Doon*, she was owned by the British Ministry of Transport, but assigned to Orient Line management. She was listed as having a peacetime capacity for 1,491 passengers, officers and troops. A mechanically troublesome ship at first, her engines were upgraded at a Southampton shipyard in 1948–49. On one previous trooping voyage, she had broken down at Port Said and had to be towed all the way home to the UK by an Admiralty tug. She also changed names in 1949, becoming the *Empire Orwell*, but still under Orient Line management. *Orwell* was selected due to Orient Line's strong preference for names beginning with 'O'. Her purpose: worldwide trooping for the British government. She was used in the Korean War as well as in the Suez Crisis of 1956 (landing troops on Cyprus and the evacuation of troops from the Suez Canal Zone). She was, however, later the subject of news-making complaints by troops about poor onboard conditions.

Her trooping days ended in 1958 when she was quickly chartered to the Karachi-based Pan-Islamic Steamship Company for a number of Muslim pilgrim voyages to and from Jeddah. This changed quickly, however, when, in November 1958, the Liverpool-headquartered Blue Funnel Line bought her and renamed her *Gunung Djati* (after a sixteenth-century Javanese poet). Refitted on the Clyde as the world's largest and finest pilgrim ship, she was fitted with an onboard mosque and an indicator that pointed towards Mecca. Another amenity was an open-air cinema and two luxury suites in the first-class section. Quarters were reset for 106 first-class passengers (in cabins) and 2,000 pilgrim passengers. Mostly, she sailed between Indonesian ports and Mecca. The Indonesian government bought the ship outright in 1962, then sold it to Indonesian owners known as the Pelni Line and then the Arafat Line, before being resold to the Indonesian government. She had a major refit and was converted to a motor ship at Hong Kong in 1973, but then was reclassified as the troop and accommodation ship *Kri Tanjung Pandan* in 1977. Laid up and decommissioned in 1986, the fifty-one-year-old vessel was scrapped at Kaohsiung on Taiwan the following year.

The twin-funnel *Empire Orwell* had been the German liner *Pretoria*. (Gillespie-Faber Collection)

EMPIRE FOWEY

Robert Stanhope joined P&O in the early 1950s and stayed with the famous shipping line for the next forty-one years. He began on a British government peacetime troopship, the *Empire Fowey*, which was managed by the Orient Line and so carried Orient Line officers, crew and even the traditional lascars on deck. 'We were carrying full loads of troops during the Malaysian wars when I was aboard,' remembered Robert.

The troops and crew like me lived in eight- and ten-bunk cabins down on the lowest decks. The voyages were long and of course very warm, but we had wind scoops for the portholes and we adjusted to the cool sea air. There was nothing like air conditioning in those days, of course. Coming back to the UK from Singapore and Penang, we carried British families and the British children that were evacuated from the war-torn areas. We also had returning soldiers and lots of wounded. The hospital aboard the *Empire Fowey* was top-flight, as good as any hospital, say, ashore in London.

'Once, we were ordered to do a thorough cleaning of the *Empire Fowey*,' concluded Robert. 'I was assigned to the oak-lined main foyer. When we lifted off the portrait of the Queen for cleaning, we found something underneath – the mounting for a Nazi eagle and swastika.'

Previously, the 634-foot-long *Potsdam* had been created for North German Lloyd's extended service between northern Europe and the Far East via the Suez Canal. Built at Hamburg and completed in the summer of 1936, the 17,528-grt ship carried only 286 passengers in two classes. Used as an accommodation ship at Hamburg in the early part of the Second World War, she was to have been rebuilt as an aircraft carrier in 1942, but this never materialized and instead she was dispatched to occupied Gdynia to serve there as an accommodation ship. Used in the mass evacuation of the Nazi-held Eastern Territories in the winter and spring of 1945, she was surrendered to the British government in May 1945 and renamed *Empire Jewel*. Later the same year, she was more extensively repaired and refitted, and renamed *Empire Fowey*. Owned by the British Ministry of Transport for peacetime trooping, she was managed by the Orient Line. Troubles followed. Within months, however, she was laid up at Glasgow with engine troubles, and later had a two-year thorough refit. Resuming service in April 1950, her accommodation was fixed as 153 first class, 94 second class, 92 third class and 1,297 troops.

Sold in March 1960, she raised the Pakistani flag for the Pan-Islamic Steamship Company as the *Safina-E-Hujjaj*. She was used primarily in Muslim pilgrim service between Karachi and Jeddah, but also sailed to East Africa and to Hong Kong. Finally withdrawn from service in February 1976, she was broken up months later, in October, at Gadani Beach in Pakistan.

Above: Another P&O-managed, peacetime trooper, the *Empire Fowey*. (Alex Duncan)

Left: Off to duty. The *Empire Fowey* departs from Southampton on a sailing to South East Asia. (P&O)

13

CANTON

Captain Philip Jackson served for a time in P&O's Far Eastern passenger service, out from London and (a day later) from Southampton via Port Said and the Suez Canal to Aden, Bombay, Colombo, Penang, Singapore, Hong Kong, Kobe and Yokohama:

> Onboard the *Canton*, I recall lots of British government, colonial and related service passengers in first class and artisans, merchants and even the odd tourist down in tourist class. We also had a very substantial inter-port business in the East, especially with Chinese and Malay passengers. I recall the traders, the plantation owners, the rubber barons.

Built at Glasgow in 1938, the 16,033-grt, handsome-looking *Canton* was a larger, improved version of the earlier *Corfu* and *Carthage*, dating from 1931. Used as an armed merchant cruiser and then a troopship during the Second World War, she resumed sailing to the Far East in October 1949. Her accommodations had by then been altered to 298 in first class and 244 in lower-deck tourist class. All first-class cabins were either single or double and eight of these rooms had private bathrooms. First-class amenities included an outdoor pool and a passenger lift.

As general liner services declined, however, ships such as the twenty-four-year-old *Canton* were less economic by 1962. That summer, upon reaching Hong Kong following her final P&O voyage, she was sold to local shipbreakers.

The *Canton* resting in the London Docks. (Michael Cassar)

A splendid painting of the *Canton* in the Thames by the late J. K. Byass. (Author's Collection)

14

ORCADES

Like P&O, the Orient Line was quick to rebuild its passenger ship fleet after heavy losses in the Second World War. In a still war-ravaged Britain, the company was allocated rationed steel by London ministers and so construction orders were given to one of the nation's finest shipbuilders, Vickers-Armstrong Limited. Large, powerful, well-equipped and very contemporary liners were ordered. The *Orcades* was the very first – she was actually ordered during the end of the war, in 1944, then had her keel laid just after the war ended, on 17 September 1945, and was due to enter service in the fall of 1947. There were delays, however, and she was not launched until October 1947, then set off on her maiden sailing to Australia over twelve months late, in December 1948. She had a unique appearance, with her bridge, wheelhouse, mast and funnel grouped close together and high above the 709-foot-long ship. Some appraisers felt she resembled a battleship while a few were convinced that she was designed for quick military conversion, should the situation arise, in those tense years of the Cold War.

After the 28,000-grt *Orcades* was delivered in December 1948, the slightly larger *Oronsay* followed in the spring of 1951, and finally a third near-sister, the *Orsova*, first appeared in spring 1954. Each ship carried some 1,400 passengers, almost equally divided between upper-deck first class and the more austere tourist class. They sailed on the well-established blue-water route for the London-headquartered Orient Line: London, Gibraltar, sometimes Naples and even Piraeus (Greece),

Port Said, Aden, Colombo, Fremantle, Melbourne and Sydney. A complete one-way trip took four weeks.

'There was a feeling in Australia that the Orient Line was slightly superior to its greatest British-flag rival, the P&O Lines,' recalled Tony Ralph.

The Orient Line staffs even felt that they were better than those on P&O liners. Orient ships also had grill rooms in first class, for example, and even charged an extra tariff for these. Also, Orient liners were decorated by Brian O'Rourke, a talented New Zealander, who used very contemporary styles. This gave the ships greater character. It was actually a very functional, but at the same time elegant, style that was actually ideally suited for the tropics.

Orient Line was innovative in other ways. 'Orient offered some of the very first cruises from Australia, even as far back as the 1930s,' added Tony Ralph.

Both P&O and Orient were really very much mainline, deep-sea companies. They rarely cruised in the Pacific, but only from the UK and within Europe. But in the 1930s, they began to experiment, making cruises from Sydney over to Auckland and Wellington, a ten-day trip in all, and later with excursions to the South Pacific islands, to the likes of Noumea and Suva.

'The full merger of the P&O and Orient lines in 1960 was said to be a difficult one for Orient Line,' added Tony Ralph. 'In fact, in 1966, the Orient name was dropped altogether and ships like the *Orcades*, *Oronsay* and *Orsova* were run thereafter as P&O liners.'

Further changes were ahead. In the massive house-cleaning in the fuel-expensive mid-1970s, this trio of fine liners found its way to all but premature endings in Far Eastern scrapyards.

As jet aircraft arrived in the late 1960s and P&O's liner operations began to face stiff competition, among other dilemmas, London-based managers had to make major decisions. There was also the problem, by the early 1970s, of an aging, less efficient fleet in an increasingly new and cost-conscious era. Furthermore, the *Orcades* had a boiler room fire while at Hong Kong in April 1972.

Captain Martin Reed was then assigned to the *Orcades*, which was twenty-four years old by 1972. 'The piping started to go on older ships like the *Orcades*,' he remembered.

We'd have fuel leaks, which required a foam-covering, and so we would have foam running about with an oil topping! We also had costly seven- to ten-day layovers for maintenance and for working cargo in the London Docks [until 1969] and later at Southampton between the long voyages. We even had two- and three-day layovers between cruises.

Laid up at Southampton in October 1972, the *Orcades* was delivered in the following winter to Nan Feng Steel Enterprises Ltd of Kaohsiung, Taiwan, for demolition.

Post-war style. With her mighty superstructure and prominent mast and funnel, the 1948-built *Orcades* was said to be a reminder of a battleship. (Roger Sherlock)

Triple grouping: *Oronsay* (left), *Canberra* (middle) and *Orcades* (right) in a 1964 view at Southampton. (H. J. Wood)

Above: Imposing, the *Orcades* was the first of a new, stylized generation of P&O-Orient liners of the late 1940s and early 1950s. (P&O-Orient)

Right: A close-up of the unique mast and funnel grouping aboard the 709-foot-long *Orcades*. (P&O)

s.s. ORCADES TOURIST CLASS 2 BERTH CABIN

Above: Orcades being broken up at Kaohsiung, Taiwan, in the winter of 1973. She was sold for one-seventh of the £3½ million she cost to build in 1947–48. (James L. Shaw)

Left: A tourist-class two-berth room cost $9 per person per day in the late 1950s for the twenty-eight days from London to Sydney. (P&O)

INSIDE (UPPER & LOWER)
DOUBLE CABIN—ORCADES

WELL APPOINTED LOUNGE,
ONE OF THE SEVERAL SPACIOUS
PUBLIC ROOMS
ON THESE SHIPS

OUTSIDE DOUBLE CABIN
(UPPER AND LOWER)

The freedom of tourist one class travel is gaining popularity — roam the whole ship — there are two swimming pools to choose from, cocktail lounges, libraries, gift shops, even a teenage hideaway

EACH SHIP HAS TWO RESTAURANTS SERVING DELIGHTFUL
CUISINE FROM ONE CENTRAL GALLEY

Above: Tourist class aboard the *Orcades*. (P&O-Orient)

Right: Orient Line voyages in the 1950s. (*Holiday* magazine)

Largest and fastest liners to Australia and New Zealand

Big-O is the way to go! You'll get a cruise mood in these trans-Pacific express liners. Fine food, fun, and flawless British service for 17-21 days. Regular Sunliner voyages from Vancouver and San Francisco via Honolulu and Fiji. Around-the-world travelers can connect in Australia for Europe, then return trans-Atlantic via Cunard. See your travel agent!

MAORI GODSTICK
Earthly abode of the god Maru, worshipped by a New Zealand cult.

ORIENT LINE
ORSOVA · ORONSAY · ORCADES · ORION
CUNARD LINE—GENERAL PASSENGER
AGENTS IN THE U.S.A. AND CANADA

HIMALAYA

In 1961, the P&O-Orient Lines, as it was then called, had a fleet of no fewer than seventeen passenger liners (plus over 400 other vessels). It was the largest, most far-flung-serving passenger fleet anywhere on earth. Mostly, P&O was still making what were called 'line voyages', carrying passengers in mostly two-class accommodations on voyages from 2 to 102 days, touching more or less regularly at over 200 ports worldwide. In the British maritime tradition of its day, P&O was based in grand headquarters, with marble interiors and wood-paneled board rooms, in London's great shipping district along Leadenhall Street. The chairman, it was said, arrived each morning at 10, in a big Rolls-Royce and with his private elevator always waiting, and took two-hour lunches and then left for the day by 4 o'clock. Tens of thousands worked for P&O on land and on sea.

When the Second World War began, P&O – like all shipowners – were busy rebuilding their fleets, restoring existing tonnage and creating replacements. P&O planned for its biggest liner yet – a highly competitive ship of some 28,000 tons, the biggest and possibly finest yet on the reviving UK–Australia run. Launched on 5 October 1948 at Barrow, the new ship was named *Himalaya*. P&O decided to give the 709-foot-long ship its own identity and therefore abandoned continuation of the Strath names. The ship's design would be different as well. There would be no mainmast. Actually, this design had been used before the war – in Orient Line's *Orion* and *Orcades*, Holland's *Oranje* and Shaw Savill's *Dominion Monarch*. Furthermore,

there were planning and accommodation changes. Instead of a balanced passenger load of approximately 500 passengers in first and in tourist class, the new ship was designed for 758 in first class and only 401 in tourist. P&O envisioned a rise in first-class traffic, namely business people, government officials, merchants and even wealthy tourists. Tourist class was for budget travelers while the migrants went to other, older P&O liners. Innovatively, the *Himalaya* was the first P&O liner to have air-conditioned cabins, although this was limited to suites and some inside rooms. Dining rooms in both classes were air conditioned.

The late Captain D. G. H. O. Baillie wrote of the *Himalaya*, 'My strong impression was the *Himalaya*'s undoubted atmosphere – she was very special. Being the first P&O liner to be built after the war and therefore a symbol to us all of returning luxury and normality, there has always been lavished on her a great deal of care, attention and affection.'

Typically, the *Himalaya* soldiered on – making Australian line voyages, cruises, trips on the expanded P&O-Orient schedules – and, by 1963, changed to a one-class liner (1,416 berths in all). In October 1969, she made the very last P&O liner sailing from London. Thereafter, all the company's passenger ships would use Southampton. It was typical of the many changes then taking place in the passenger liner industry.

Mick Harper joined the famed shipping line in 1961 as a so-called utility steward. For $60 a month, he was posted to the

Himalaya. 'I did everything – but mostly I worked in what we called "the plate house", that part of the ship's galley where we did the washing-up. I was a "plate washer".'

He added,

It was tough, hard work and, when finished, the dishes from the passenger restaurants were red hot. But for years, it seems that the plate washers would toss lots of dishes and silver as well out the galley portholes so as not to have to wash them. It was jokingly said that there were enough P&O dishes on the seabed that you could walk all the way from London to Sydney. But by the time I joined, the company placed metal mesh screens over the galley portholes to stop the tossing.

Harper also recalled, 'We also carried lots of British immigrants, who paid $40 for the four-week voyage out to Australia, on these voyages.' Some 100,000 Brits left home shores for new, hopefully better lives abroad. Australia was most welcoming at the time and so a very popular destination. P&O liners outbound for ports down under were usually full-up.

They were usually poor people, sometimes very poor people, going to places like Melbourne and Sydney to begin new lives. But sometimes they had strange ways. They often used to steal the silverware onboard the ships, for example, and so there were often too few or even no spoons by the time we reached Sydney. In the end, there were waiters who kept a spoon tied to a string to their jackets and then they'd stir everyone's tea or coffee. Of course, there weren't many big tippers down in the bottom end of tourist class and the waiters used to sell sets of the voyage menus to the immigrants for 50 cents.

Inevitably, it all gradually began to change by the late 1960s. Passengers were taking to the skies, using airlines, and the two-class ocean liner business was turning into the one-class cruise business. 'Once, by the mid-1960s, on a voyage home to London from Sydney, we had only three passengers [out of 750] in first class aboard the *Himalaya*. I saw the writing on the wall and left the sea, but the sea left me with some great memories,' concluded Mick Harper.

Finishing her P&O career as a cruise ship sailing from Sydney, the *Himalaya* had a huge send-off on a final, one-way cruise up to Hong Kong in October 1974. After landing her passengers, she sailed empty over to Taiwan and was delivered to local scrappers on 28 November.

A popular ship, the handsome *Himalaya*. (Luis Miguel Correia)

A P&O threesome in the London Docks: *Himalaya* (left), *Chusan* (center) and *Canton* (right). (P&O)

The 709-foot-long *Himalaya* outward bound in the Thames. (B. Reeves)

A postcard of the *Himalaya* and her classic, post-war interiors. (Lindsay Johnson Collection)

Himalaya

28,000 TONS

Fully Air-conditioned and Stabilized

bears the name of the famous range of mountains forming the northern boundary of India and Pakistan. Built in 1949 with accommodations for 1416 one class tourist passengers, and a crew of 631 She is 709 feet long, 91 feet wide and has a speed of 22 knots.

SHELTERED DECKS FOR LOUNGING AND READING

FRIENDS ENJOY A CHAT AND A DRINK IN THE MAIN LOUNGE

Accommodation aboard the *Himalaya*. (P&O)

FOUR BERTH CABIN WITH SHOWER—ORCADES

OUTSIDE THREE BERTH CABIN WITH BATH —HIMALAYA

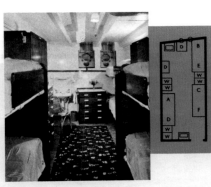

OUTSIDE SIX BERTH CABIN

OUTSIDE FOUR BERTH CABIN—HIMALAYA

Cabins aboard the *Himalaya* and the similar *Orcades*. (P&O)

DINNER

Appetizers	Orange Juice	Mortadella Sausage	Pineapple Seafood Cocktail
Soups	Consommé Printanière Royale		Cream of Tomato

Main Courses

Poached Fillet of Halibut, Florentine
(Served on a bed of Spinach covered with Cheese Sauce, glazed)

Roast Chicken, Sage and Onion Dressing, Bread Sauce

Roast Ribs of Beef, Yorkshire Pudding, Horseradish Cream

Grilled Lamb Cutlet, Creamed Potatoes, Minted Green Peas

Vegetables	Buttered Brussels Sprouts		Lima Beans
Potatoes	Parmentier	Roast	Boiled

Cold Buffet, Salads and Dressings

Ham	Roast Beef	Roast Lamb
Loin of Veal		Preserved Beef

Mixed Fresh and Tossed Green Salads

Mayonnaise, French and Vinaigrette Dressings

Sweets	Vienna Pudding	Apricot Femina

Strawberry Ice Cream

Cheese

Cheddar	Danish Blue	Edam
Double Gloucester	Stilton	

Biscuits

Sao Crackers	Vita-Weat	Jatz Crackers
Thin Captain	Ryvita	

Fresh Fruit	Apples	Oranges	Passion Fruit
Beverages	Coffee	Instant Coffee	Tea

After Dinner Mints

Tea and Coffee are also served in Public Rooms

CHEF   Denis J Rogers

HIMALAYA

Saturday 19 October, 1974

Above: The cover of a P&O-Orient cruising brochure, 1964. (P&O)

Left: Dinner menu from the *Himalaya*'s last voyage in October 1974. (Lindsay Johnson Collection)

The *Himalaya* departing from Sydney with the *Canberra* on the right. (Lindsay Johnson Collection)

16

CHUSAN

'Back in the 1960s, it was often said at P&O, and by passengers as well as crew, that the *Chusan* was the absolute best ship in the fleet,' remembered Howard Franklin, who sailed just about all the P&O-Orient liners of that era. 'It was said that the *Chusan* was the best-built, best-run and the friendliest liner in the entire fleet.'

'My favorite P&O liner in the 1950s was the *Chusan*,' recalled Robert Eldridge.

She was not used on the well-known service to Australia, but was assigned to the P&O's Far East service – London–Suez–Bombay–Singapore–Hong Kong–Japan run. It took four months to make a round trip. The *Chusan*, at 24,000 tons and carrying up to 1,000 passengers, was slightly smaller than, say, the *Himalaya*, *Arcadia* and *Iberia*. The *Chusan* had something special – a warmth and nice, friendly feeling about her. She might have looked like the others, but she was different and other P&O passengers and crew felt the same. On the *Chusan*, we made P&O's very first world cruise, well world voyage. The year was 1958, as I remember. We sailed out to Hong Kong and then on to Kobe and Yokohama, but instead of reversing and heading home to London, we crossed the Pacific to Honolulu and then to Los Angeles and San Francisco. We then sailed up to Vancouver and then went off on a two-week cruise to Hawaii, returned to California and then sailed home to London, stopping at Acapulco, the Panama Canal and the Caribbean. On that leg, and for the first time aboard the *Chusan*, we had more American than British passengers onboard.

P&O wanted to develop, to cultivate, the American West Coast passenger and tourist market.

Commissioned in the late summer of 1950, the *Chusan* was designed purposely as P&O's biggest and finest liner but on the Far Eastern run from London. She was paired with the smaller *Corfu*, *Carthage* and *Canton*.

Martin Reed, later Captain Reed, joined P&O as a 'career company', hoping to be placed aboard one of their 'big white liners': 'I actually joined P&O in 1961, after applying at their grand offices at 122 Leadenhall Street in London,' he remembered.

After serving aboard P&O freighters as well as tankers, Martin Reed was finally assigned to the liners – to the *Chusan* and then the *Iberia*. He served as a cadet aboard the *Chusan* and remembered, 'Cadets usually drove the ship's tenders. It was two-class travel for line voyages and even for cruising back then: comfortable, spacious first class and less expensive, rather basic tourist class. First-class passengers went ashore first, of course. It was the British class system, but on the sea.'

'Onboard the *Chusan* and the other P&O Australia-routed liners, we called at Bombay very often on the way from or to England,' added Captain Reed.

In first class, we would have wealthy businessmen, relieving ambassadors and consul generals, and also Indian princes and Middle Eastern sheiks with their entourages and even harems.

The Eastern royalties took blocks of cabins and traveled with their own, sword-carrying guards. We would be completely full in tourist class with British immigrants going out to resettle in Australia and with budget-conscious tourists and some unhappy, disgruntled, reverse immigrants on the way back.

Ships like the *Chusan* also had large cargo capacities, usually up to six deep holds. 'These liners were also huge cargo carriers,' he noted. 'We would have general, British-made manufactured goods going out and refrigerated items like meat as well as some wool from Australia. We also picked up the cheap produce of the Orient, at ports such as Hong Kong and Singapore.'

P&O had British officers but, in a reflection of their colonial past, mostly Indian crews. 'It was a sort of family amongst the British staff on P&O liners back then,' Reed recalled.

There was [sic] always two officers on watch, for example, and a huge, ongoing rivalry with the officers aboard the Orient Line passenger ships. Stewards and waiters in the passenger areas were Goan from India. They were all English speaking, came from that former Portuguese colony in north-west India and as many as 99 per cent were Roman Catholic. There was always a big shrine in the Goan mess.

'It was all quite different, even for cruising, back then,' he added.

Passenger entertainment was minimal by today's standards. A so-called Liaison Officer was the Entertainment or Cruise Director for each class and he formed a ship/passenger committee that organized events, mostly for the evenings. The company did provide a band or two for dancing, however.

Otherwise, after-dinner activities were quite simple: fancy dress, horse-racing, games and quizzes.

In May 1973, David Carr was among the eighty crew members who took the 24,200-grt *Chusan* out to the shipbreakers at Kaohsiung on Taiwan.

We sailed from Southampton to Hong Kong via Dakar, Durban and Singapore. When we reached Taiwan, there was simply no space at the Kaohsiung scrapyards so we were ordered, by P&O in London, to temporarily wait at Hong Kong, just off Green Island and next to the wreckage of the *Seawise University*, the former *Queen Elizabeth*. We sat there for a week. It was a haunting wait – the fire-gutted, sunken former *Elizabeth* and the empty, death-bound *Chusan*.

'The voyage out to the East in the *Chusan* was really quite bizarre,' added Carr.

She was – like other P&O liners on their way to the boneyards – completely stripped. The officers sat at the two surviving tables in the corner of the former first-class restaurant. There were still white linens on the table, but otherwise the room itself was empty, like a steel barn. There was nothing left.

When we were finally cleared to take the *Chusan* into Kaohsiung harbor, I shall always remember the sight along the riverbanks. Ships lined both sides, all tightly squeezed together and mostly secured stern-first. They were each waiting for demolition crews that would finish them off. We were finally berthed next to an American freighter, but were temporarily moored to buoys rather than being deliberately run aground, which was so often the case with the other liners.

'We had to wait for several days aboard the *Chusan* until London signaled that the final payment for the ship had been made,' concluded David Carr.

I remember sailing back down the river at Kaohsiung in a launch and spotting an inbound tug towing a long, flat, double-bottom and protruding piece of bow. I noticed the name *Orcades*. It was the remains of yet another early P&O liner. Her last pieces were being towed upriver to be blown up.

The *Chusan* as seen off Le Havre from the *Rotterdam*. (Author's Collection)

A postcard of the *Chusan* and her passenger spaces. (Lindsay Johnson Collection)

End of the line. The laid-up *Chusan* at Southampton in May 1973, with the *S A Vaal* and *Edinburgh Castle* on the left. (Steffen Weirauch Collection)

S.S. "CHUSAN"

Mediterranean Cruise

July 4th, — July 18th 1953

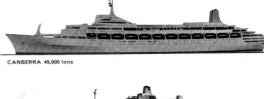

CANBERRA 45,000 tons

ORIANA 42,000 tons

ARCADIA 30,000 tons

IBERIA 30,000 tons

ORSOVA 29,000 tons

CHUSAN 24,000 tons

All these cruise ships are air-conditioned and are fitted with anti-roll stabilisers

---

A souvenir log from the *Chusan*, July 1953. (Author's Collection)   The P&O-Orient cruising fleet in the 1960s. (Author's Collection)

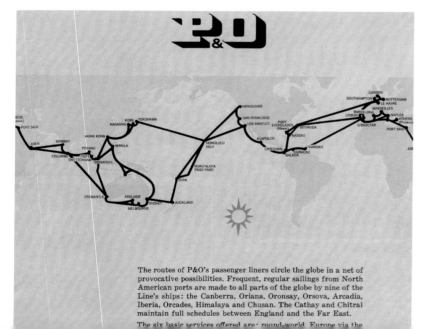

OUTHAMPTON TO GIBRALTAR — 1151 MILES		
	TIME	DATE
eparture Southampton	5.14 p.m.	July 4th
hrough Bay of Biscay	00.26 a.m.	,, 6th
assed : C. St. Vincent	7.32 p.m.	,, 6th
rrival Gibraltar	7.26 a.m.	,, 7th
Days best run —	474 miles at 19.75 knots	
Highest Temperature : 76F, 4 p.m. July 6th		

RHODES TO PALERMO — 771 MILES		
	TIME	DATE
Departure Rhodes	6.13 p.m.	July 11th
Through Kithera Channel	6.13 p.m.	,, 12th
Through Messina Straits	1.00 a.m.	,, 13th
Arrival Palermo	7.37 a.m.	,, 13th
Days best run —	500 miles at 20.83 knots	
Highest Temperature : 87F, 4p.m. July 13th		

GIBRALTAR TO RHODES — 1707 MILES		
	TIME	DATE
eparture Gibraltar	1.05 p.m.	July 7th
assed Malta	3.00 p.m.	,, 9th
,, Crete	6.00 p.m.	,, 10th
rrival Rhodes	71.4 a.m.	,, 11th
Days best run —	459 miles at 20.18 knots	
Highest Temperature : 82F, 4 p.m. July 11th		

PALERMO TO TILBURY — 2223 MILES		
	TIME	DATE
Departure Palermo	5.03 p.m.	July 13th
Passed Gibraltar	12.30 p.m.	,, 15th
Through Bay of Biscay	10.00 a.m.	,, 17th
Arrival Tilbury	10.00 a.m.	,, 18th
Days best run —	507 miles at 21.13 knots	
Highest Temperature : 87F, 4 p.m. July 13th		

TOTAL MILEAGE — 5852

Above: The good-looking *Chusan* passing under Sydney Harbour Bridge. (Lindsay Johnson Collection)

Top left: The log from that July 1953 Mediterranean cruise aboard the *Chusan*. (Author's Collection)

Left: P&O worldwide passenger map from the 1950s. (P&O)

The routes of P&O's passenger liners circle the globe in a net of provocative possibilities. Frequent, regular sailings from North American ports are made to all parts of the globe by nine of the Line's ships: the Canberra, Oriana, Oronsay, Orsova, Arcadia, Iberia, Orcades, Himalaya and Chusan. The Cathay and Chitral maintain full schedules between England and the Far East.

The six basic services offered are: round-world, Europe via the

Chusan

24,000 TONS

Fully Air-conditioned and Stabilized

is named after an archipelago off the coast of south east Asia. She has accommodations for 455 first class and 541 tourist class passengers with a crew of 556. CHUSAN, built in 1950, is the second P&O-Orient liner to carry the name, cruises at 22 knots, has a length of 673 feet and breadth of 85 feet.

THE SHIP'S SHOPS IN EACH CLASS FEATURE INTERNATIONAL BARGAINS THIS ONE IS FIRST CLASS

THERE IS AMPLE DECK SPACE FIRST & TOURIST FOR OUTDOOR SPORTS ALSO A SWIMMING POOL FOR EACH CLASS

THE BALLROOM IN FIRST CLASS IS THE SCENE OF MANY A GALA PARTY

THE TOURIST CLASS LOUNGE IS A QUIET PLACE FOR READING OR JUST SOCIALIZING

RESTAURANT FIRST CLASS EQUIPPED TO SERVE THREE MEALS A DAY IN TWO SITTINGS

THE LOUNGE IN FIRST CLASS—CHEERFUL & BRIGHT

The *Chusan* and her accommodations. (P&O-Orient)

Quarters aboard the *Chusan*. (P&O-Orient)

17

ORONSAY

Built initially for Orient Line's UK–Australia trade, it was the 28,136-grt *Oronsay* that had, in fact, opened up the Pacific for the combined P&O and Orient Lines service up from Sydney to San Francisco in 1954. Afterward, the 709-foot-long liner sailed around the world.

A modified version of the earlier *Orcades*, the *Oronsay* was actually very nearly destroyed by a fire at Vickers' yard at Barrow on 28 October 1950. Flooded with firefighters' water, she later capsized partially. She was saved, however, then repaired and – praises to the shipyard crews – was barely late for her maiden sailing in April 1951.

Like most liners, the *Oronsay* had her share of notations. In July 1967, while homeward bound in the Pacific, the ship had a fire while at sea and had to be brought into Hong Kong for inspection and repairs. There were no casualties, but forty-three tourist-class cabins suffered smoke damage, and their occupants shifted to alternate quarters.

In January 1970, the *Oronsay* made headlines around the world when she was quarantined at Vancouver with sixty-nine confirmed cases of typhoid on board. The liner, anchored in the outer harbor, was held in that Canadian port for over a month before being allowed to continue on her way, by which time 390 passengers had either canceled their trip entirely or found other means of transport.

By 1971, as the old line services were in steady decline, the *Oronsay* was made one class for all but full-time cruising – from Southampton in summer and from Sydney for the remainder of the year. Although quite successful, her age was increasingly against her. In April 1975, with her twenty-five-year survey pending, P&O announced that the *Oronsay* was to be retired. In September, she made a farewell cruise – one-way from Sydney to Hong Kong. From there, she crossed to Kaohsiung on Taiwan and was handed over to the Nan Feng Steel Enterprise Co. for breaking. In the course of her twenty-four years of service, the *Oronsay* had called at 150 ports, making sixty-four line voyages and thirty-seven cruises.

'Ships such as the *Oronsay* had gone from traditional line voyages to cruising,' remembered Captain Ian Tompkins. 'The *Oronsay* had lost her passengers on regular voyages to and from Australia as well as her cargo. Even the far newer *Canberra* might have gone [in late 1973] to the breakers. The price of fuel oil was the decisive if not final blow to these liners.'

Oronsay deck plan. (P&O-Orient)

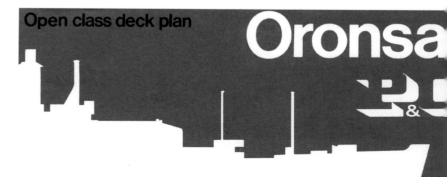

Open class deck plan
Oronsa...
P&O

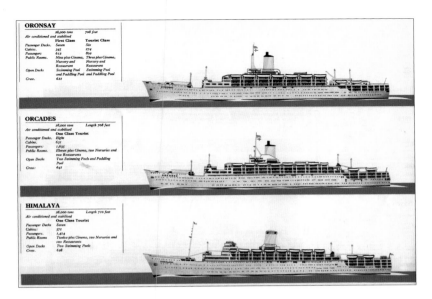

ORONSAY
28,000 tons · 708 feet
Air conditioned and stabilized

	First Class	Tourist Class
Passenger Decks:	Seven	Six
Cabins:	345	274
Passengers:	612	802
Public Rooms:	Nine plus Cinema, Nursery and Restaurant	Three plus Cinema, Nursery and Restaurant
Open Decks:	Swimming Pool and Paddling Pool	Swimming Pool and Paddling Pool
Crew:	621	

ORCADES
28,000 tons · Length 708 feet
Air conditioned and stabilized
One Class Tourist

Passenger Decks:	Eight
Cabins:	631
Passengers:	1,635
Public Rooms:	Eleven plus Cinema, two Nurseries and two Restaurants
Open Decks:	Two Swimming Pools and Paddling Pool
Crew:	641

HIMALAYA
28,000 tons · Length 710 feet
Air conditioned and stabilized
One Class Tourist

Passenger Decks:	Seven
Cabins:	571
Passengers:	1,414
Public Rooms:	Twelve plus Cinema, two Nurseries and two Restaurants
Open Decks:	Two Swimming Pools
Crew:	628

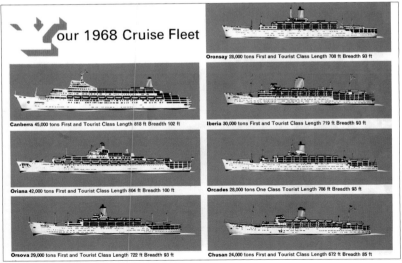

our 1968 Cruise Fleet

Oronsay 28,000 tons First and Tourist Class Length 708 ft Breadth 93 ft

Canberra 45,000 tons First and Tourist Class Length 818 ft Breadth 102 ft

Iberia 30,000 tons First and Tourist Class Length 719 ft Breadth 93 ft

Oriana 42,000 tons First and Tourist Class Length 804 ft Breadth 100 ft

Orcades 28,000 tons One Class Tourist Length 708 ft Breadth 93 ft

Orsova 29,000 tons First and Tourist Class Length 722 ft Breadth 93 ft

Chusan 24,000 tons First and Tourist Class Length 672 ft Breadth 85 ft

The British Cruise Line

Cherry Blossom Circle Pacific Cruise

S.S. Oronsay · March 1973

Top left: The *Oronsay* and the similar *Orcades* and *Himalaya*. (P&O)

Left: The *Oronsay* is included in P&O's cruising fleet in 1968. (P&O)

Right: Cruise brochure, 1973. (Andrew Kilk Collection)

Oronsay

28,000 TONS

Fully Air-conditioned and Stabilized

takes her name from one of the islands of the Hebrides, west of Scotland. Built in 1951 with accommodations for 614 first class and 804 tourist class passengers, she has a crew of 635. Her length is 709 feet long, her breadth 93 feet, and her speed 22 knots.

Unloading. The *Oronsay* at Hong Kong. (James L. Shaw Collection)

THE FRIENDLY ATMOSPHERE OF A FIRST CLASS LOUNGE

TOURIST CLASS RESTAURANT READY FOR THE NEXT MEAL
ALWAYS AN INTERESTING TREAT

Welcome aboard! The *Oronsay* and her accommodations. (P&O)

Below: Los Angeles harbor. The *Oronsay* meets the *Canberra*. (P&O)

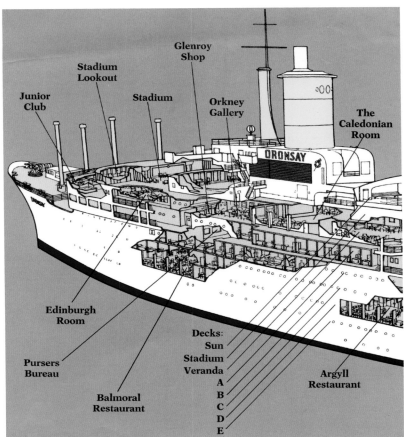

Junior Club

Stadium Lookout

Glenroy Shop

Stadium

Orkney Gallery

The Caledonian Room

ORONSAY

Edinburgh Room

Pursers Bureau

Balmoral Restaurant

Decks:
Sun
Stadium
Veranda
A
B
C
D
E

Argyll Restaurant

A partial cutaway relief of the 28,000-grt *Oronsay*. (P&O)

18

ARCADIA

As part of the large post-war rebuilding program, P&O added new liners, namely the 28,000-grt *Himalaya* in 1948, the 24,000-grt *Chusan* in 1950 and finally, biggest of all, the 29,000-grt near-sisters *Arcadia* and *Iberia* in 1954. They were created especially as the lead ships for the company's booming trade between London, Melbourne and Sydney.

The *Arcadia* was one of P&O's most popular and beloved liners. She and her near-sister *Iberia* were ordered in 1952 as the culmination of the company's post-war liner rebuilding program. The ships were, however, ordered from different shipbuilders: the *Arcadia* from John Brown & Co. at Clydebank (builders of the three big Cunard Queens among many others) and the *Iberia* from Harland & Wolff at Belfast (creators of the *Titanic* and, later, the equally large *Canberra*). The only other, more apparent difference was that the two ships were fitted with different funnels: the *Arcadia*'s was domed and had a black-painted top whereas the *Iberia*'s was curved and had some open grating.

The 721-foot-long *Arcadia* carried some 1,390 passengers – divided almost evenly between a pleasant, very comfortable first class (655 berths) and a more austere, less expensive tourist class (735 berths). They were quite big liners, equivalent to many of the more notable Atlantic liners such as the *America*, *Andrea Doria* and *Caronia*. The *Arcadia* was launched on 14 May 1953, ironically the same day as the Orient Line's new flagship and largest liner, the *Orsova*. This latter ship was built, however, at the Vickers yard in Barrow-in-Furness. After

launching, the *Arcadia* was moved to a fitting-out berth and sat alongside another incomplete ship, the royal yacht *Britannia*, which was to be presented to a young Queen Elizabeth II as a Coronation present from the Royal Navy.

The *Arcadia* entered service in February 1954, sailing from London's Tilbury Docks (after loading cargo) and then the Landing Stage (for passengers) to Gibraltar, Port Said, Aden, Colombo, Fremantle, Melbourne and Sydney. In addition to their line voyages to Australia, these ships occasionally went cruising – for example, on two- and three-week itineraries to the Mediterranean or to the Atlantic isles, Spain and Portugal, or on more exotic itineraries such as three weeks across the Atlantic to New York and other Atlantic ports in 1959. Both ships began sailing more regularly on worldwide patterns soon after P&O merged its liner services with the Orient Line in 1960. The *Arcadia* made P&O's first cruises to Alaska in the late 1960s.

With her polished veneers, brasswork, soft chairs and expansive open-air deck spaces, she quickly established a special, long-lasting rapport with her passengers and her crew. Rather strangely, the *Iberia* never quite had the same charmed relationship with the traveling public. One *Arcadia* loyalist later reported, 'She was a ship of tremendous charm and personality. Actually, that charm is a certain, undefinable something that pervades throughout certain ships, very few of them in fact, and which lingers in the most beautiful, evocative memories. The *Arcadia* was always my absolute favorite.'

Howard Franklin began sailing (and later speaking as a guest lecturer) aboard P&O liners in the 1970s, beginning in the last golden years of the line and those extensive world voyages, and then later on cruises aboard P&O. He has made countless voyages. 'The *Arcadia* was positively my favorite P&O ship back then,' he said.

She was so inviting, friendly, even cozy. She had club chairs in the library, for example, and you could curl up and read a good book. P&O ships differed from Orient Line ships. P&O had more equalitarian styles onboard. There was less aristocracy in first class than aboard the Orient Line ships, for example.

Tony Ralph, an enthusiastic observer of ocean liners at Auckland and at Sydney, made his very first P&O cruise aboard the *Arcadia* in 1966. A short cruise, the sailing was from Auckland to Pitcairn and the Tin Can islands. 'She was a great ship with a colonial country club style,' he recalled. 'She was lighter in style than, say, the earlier *Himalaya*. The *Arcadia* got away from the traditional dark woods favored by P&O for their earlier passenger ships. There was indirect lighting and ceiling designs aboard the *Arcadia* as well.'

Life aboard was quite different, as Tony Ralph remembered, from, say, today's entertainment and amenity-filled cruise ships:

On the *Arcadia*, after dinner in the restaurant, coffee was served in the lounge and was very much a separate event. There were lots of conversational areas in the lounges and so you tended to meet more passengers over the course of a voyage. Formal entertainment was minimal. A film was the only offering on some nights. Then there was an Easter parade of hats, frog racing and tombola on others. Cabaret shows were unheard of back then and a spirited disco on an aft, open deck was a big, well-attended event! There was no television or radio in the cabins on the *Arcadia* so that reading the printed news sheets was an activity in itself.

Long retired, Henry Gibbons spent twenty years, beginning in 1957, with P&O, mostly as a dining room waiter. He mainly served aboard the *Arcadia*. 'She was a great ship, perhaps my favorite at P&O, and had a friendly onboard feel,' he remembered.

We sailed about nine months of the year on the UK–Australia run, down to Fremantle, Melbourne and Sydney. We usually went out by way of the Suez Canal, but sometimes went completely around the world as a return, using Panama. Up in first class, we had lots of elegant, posh passengers – businessmen, government people, up-market tourists. But down in tourist, it was a different story, much like another world. We carried lots and lots of 'Ten Pound Poms', very simple British families going out to Australia to resettle. Many of them were very poor and some had never been served a meal in their entire lives. They were sometimes very short on manners, rarely tipped and had a sense of fear in heading off to the unknown down under. Sometimes, in tourist class, we'd have several hundred children aboard but many could be quite unruly and misbehaved. They turned tourist class into a playground and sometimes tried their hand at slipping into first class. Then for the remaining three months of the year, the *Arcadia* would go cruising, two classes in those days, from Southampton and sometimes from Sydney. The British cruise passengers tended to be older and even genteel whereas the Australians were younger, loud and noisy and wanted to party day after day. So, in the course of a year, a ship like the *Arcadia* had many different types of passengers – and so many different moods.

Daily life had its rituals, which were a part of P&O-Orient's seagoing culture. According to Tony Ralph,

A cup of tea and a biscuit was served in the cabins to all passengers each morning. This was a pre-breakfast tradition. Lunch was always offered in the restaurant whereas a buffet lunch on deck was considered a special event and might be offered only once during a voyage. Everyone was very punctual at mealtimes, especially at dinner. Travel by ship, even by the 1960s, was still very special to Australians and New Zealanders. It was all very ritualized.

Captain Nick Carlton also remembered the 22-knot, steam turbine-driven *Arcadia*. He served aboard her in the mid-1970s. 'We made a Vancouver–Sydney voyage in preparation for the ship being based full-time in Australia for one-class cruising,' he noted.

She was a lovely, very traditional ship. We would have three-day layovers in some ports and ran at high speeds, burning huge amounts of fuel. There was lots of excess spending in those days. P&O ran the bars and the bingo, and so there was lots of theft by the crew. There were still full Union crews at the time, wages were high and some cabin stewards received such massive tips from passengers that they actually signed off and flew home in mid voyage. Ships like the *Arcadia* were also very solid. We will never see that standard of construction again.

As P&O disposed of its post-war liners in the early 1970s, it was in fact her near-sister, the *Iberia*, that was the first to go to the breakers (in 1972). After 1976, the much loved *Arcadia* was the sole survivor of this generation of liners from the late 1940s and early 1950s. She had something as a reprieve and was used in Pacific cruising from Sydney until early 1979. Then, she too made a final run up to Taiwan to meet the inevitable breakers. However, unlike most other P&O liners, the *Arcadia* was not completely stripped for her final voyage. She was leaving behind

a fine record, completing twenty-five years of very successful service.

James Shaw, a noted American maritime journalist, went aboard the ship at Kaohsiung in March 1979. He later wrote,

At the time of my visit, the *Arcadia* was positioned alongside the 99,400-ton Greek tanker *Andros Apollon* as the P&O ship's berth was not yet available. At that time, stripping operations of the *Arcadia* were in progress. Furniture and bedding were being lowered over the side and being taken ashore in two lifeboats. Two other lifeboats were being used as 'tankers' to take off her excess fuel oil. The same fuel oil would be used to heat [a] ships' plate in furnaces ashore so that it could be formed into steel reinforcement bars.

'Onboard the *Arcadia*, Taiwanese work crews were already engaged in taking up the hardwood decks aft,' wrote Shaw.

The carpeting in most public rooms had been cut and rolled up. The officers' cabins on the bridge and the chartroom had already been stripped of most equipment. The radio room and all radio instruments had been sealed by local Government inspectors.

Most 'nautical antiques' – such as the large P&O world map from the aft bar and the line drawing in wood of the *Arcadia* on B Deck – had been removed by the Rainbow Enterprise Company. This firm, based in Kaohsiung, bought the interior decorations of liners that had come to Taiwan for breaking-up. The items were then exported to nautical shops around the world. As for the ship itself, I was told that she was purchased at the market rate of $100 per light displacement ton (the *Arcadia* was 23,060 light displacement tons), which came to approximately $2.5 million. It would take eight to ten weeks to complete dismantling of the *Arcadia*.

Arcadia

30,000 TONS

Fully Air-conditioned and Stabilized

takes her name from the country in ancient Greece. Cut off by mountains from the outside world, the inhabitants who led a quiet life, were known as "Arcadian." The ARCADIA built in 1954 is the second P&O ship of this name and carries 647 first class and 735 tourist class passengers with a crew of 711 She cruises at 22 knots, is 720 feet long and 91 feet wide.

THE VERANDAH CAFE AFT ON THE PROMENADE DECK OPENS ON THE FIRST CLASS SWIMMING POOL

FIRST CLASS OBSERVATION LOUNGE SITUATED FORWARD OFFERS PANORAMIC VIEW OF THE SEA AHEAD

Cheers! The launch of the *Arcadia* on 14 May 1953 at the John Brown yard at Clydebank. (P&O)

The highly popular *Arcadia* and her passenger spaces. (P&O)

The *Arcadia* arrives at New York for the first and only time in this view dated 21 September 1959. (Moran Towing & Transportation Co.)

The maiden voyage of the mighty *Arcadia*. (Cronican-Arroyo Collection)

Portuguese rendezvous. The *Arcadia* and *Canberra* at Lisbon. (Luis Miguel Correia)

Right: Outward bound. The *Arcadia* departing Sydney. (P&O)

Left: Summer cruising. During a Northern Cities cruise, the *Arcadia* is seen at Hamburg. (Cronican-Arroyo Collection)

Arcadia / Iberia

A SUNNY STROLL ALONG THE PROMENADE DECK

THE LIBRARY IN FIRST CLASS

THERE IS A SWIMMING POOL IN EACH CLASS
ALWAYS A BUSY PLACE ON A WARM AFTERNOON

TOURIST CLASS PASSENGERS HAVE THEIR OWN SPACIOU...
WITH VIEW WINDOWS

TOURIST CLASS RESTAURANT

TOURIST CLASS PASSENGERS ENJOY
THE VAST DECK SPACE

FIRST CLASS RESTAURANT

A SMALL QU ET WRITING ROOM IN FIRST CLASS

Accommodations aboard the *Arcadia* and her near-sister *Iberia*. (P&O)

Additional passenger spaces aboard the *Arcadia* and *Iberia*. (P&O)

Iberia/Arcadia

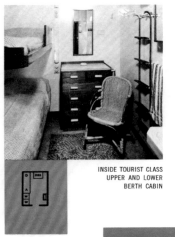

THIS SPACIOUS DELUXE
FIRST CLASS CABIN HAS LARGE
SEA VIEW WINDOWS

INSIDE TOURIST CLASS
UPPER AND LOWER
BERTH CABIN

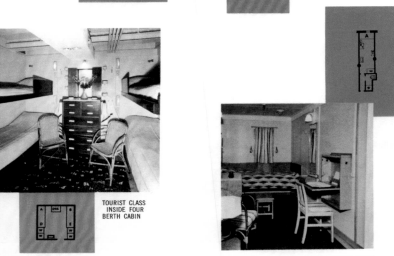

TOURIST CLASS
INSIDE FOUR
BERTH CABIN

COMFORTABLE OUTSIDE SINGLE BERTH
CABIN WITH SHOWER IN FIRST CLASS

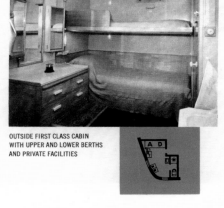

OUTSIDE FIRST CLASS CABIN
WITH UPPER AND LOWER BERTHS
AND PRIVATE FACILITIES

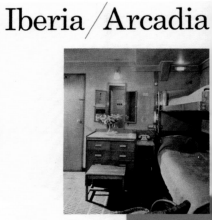

INSIDE FIRST CLASS
UPPER AND LOWER
BERTH CABIN
WITH SHOWER

LARGE OUTSIDE
FIRST CLASS TWIN BEDDED
CABIN WITH BATHROOM

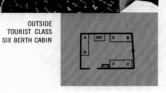

OUTSIDE
TOURIST CLASS
SIX BERTH CABIN

First-class cabins aboard the *Arcadia*. (P&O)

Less expensive tourist-class cabins. (P&O)

LUNCHEON

SCOTCH BROTH

FRIED HAKE, RÉMOULADE SAUCE

STEAK AND KIDNEY PUDDING

MACARONI MILANAISE

VEGETABLES

POTATOES:	BOILED	CREAMED
	BRUSSELS SPROUTS	

COLD SIDEBOARD

PRESERVED BRISKET	GAME PIE

SALAD

MIXED SALAD

SWEETS

FRESH STRAWBERRIES WITH CREAM	COFFEE ICE

CHEESES

TAFFEL	DANISH BLUE
BISCUITS	COFFEE

TEA AND COFFEE IS SERVED IN ALL PUBLIC ROOMS

A VEGETARIAN MENU IS AVAILABLE ON REQUEST TO THE HEAD WAITER OR DEPUTY PURSER

S.S. "ARCADIA"   FRIDAY, 16TH JUNE, 1961

Tourist-class deck plan aboard the *Arcadia*, dated 1962. (Andrew Kilk Collection)

Cruising the Pacific – two months for $1,600! (Andrew Kilk Collection)

Tourist-class luncheon menu aboard the *Arcadia*, dated 16 June 1961 (Lindsay Johnson Collection)

Above: During the otherwise devastating British maritime strike in May–June 1966, the *Canberra* (left) and *Arcadia* are 'nested' together awaiting their return to service. (P&O)

Right: Arrival at Suva. The majestic *Arcadia* makes an early morning arrival. (P&O)

Pacific Cruises 1977

FARES EFFECTIVE 24th. JAN.
SUPERSEDES ALL PREVIOUS ISSUES

Let yourself go with P&O

Above: Berthed at Vancouver. (Albert Wilhelmi Collection)

Left: Final years. The *Arcadia* cruised full-time from Sydney in the late 1970s. (P&O)

19

IBERIA

Following the merger with the Orient Line in 1960, the *Iberia* – like most other P&O liners – began making worldwide voyages. Itineraries increased to calls at over 100 world ports. In the early 1960s, as an example, the *Iberia* made a 120-day voyage that took her from Southampton to Gibraltar, Naples, Piraeus, Suez, Aden, Bombay, Colombo, Fremantle, Melbourne, Sydney, Singapore, Hong Kong, Kobe, Yokohama, Honolulu, Vancouver, San Francisco, Los Angeles, Acapulco, the Panama Canal, Curaçao, Fort Lauderdale, Nassau, and Bermuda before returning to Southampton. Fares ranged from $15 per person per day in first class to $9 in tourist class. Some passengers made the full trip, others sailed outward to Australia, others crossed the Pacific and still others made short two- to three-day passages.

Built by Harland & Wolff at Belfast and completed in September 1954, the *Iberia* was a very handsome-looking liner. She differed from her near-sister *Arcadia* by having a different funnel design. The *Iberia* was, however, a problematic ship – she had, for example, mechanical woes for most of her life. In the late sixties, P&O actually thought of re-engining the ship, but the rising prices of fuel oil canceled all plans. Also, in March 1956, the *Iberia* was badly damaged in a collision in the Indian Ocean with the tanker *Stanvac Pretoria*. The *Iberia* suffered serious port side damages and required seventeen days of repairs once at Sydney.

In the diverse, far-flung P&O-Orient fleet, David Carr gained his 2nd mate's ticket in late 1963, and then joined the *Iberia*.

I made the special cruise in her from Los Angeles to Yokohama for the 1964 Olympic Games at Tokyo. There were all sorts of cruises to Japan that year, many of them in P&O liners. In those days, a P&O voyage might last as long as five months. We'd sail out to Australia from the UK, then go up to Hong Kong and Japan, then down to Australia again and then finally home to England by way of Ceylon, the Suez and the Med. Of course, there were many alternates as well. After the Suez Canal closed in 1967, we were routed via South Africa. Also, we almost always stopped at either Bombay or Colombo for Indian crew changes. During these years, I must have been King Neptune at least a dozen times.

Captain Bob Ellingham was witness to the great disposal of most of the post-war P&O liners in the early 1970s to the scrapyards of Taiwan. '*Iberia* started them off in June 1972,' he recalled.

She was then only eighteen years old, but the most troublesome of the lot. She was always a problematic ship. Actually, none of that immediate post-war group – *Orcades, Himalaya, Chusan, Oronsay, Arcadia, Iberia* and *Orsova* – were destined to see the age of thirty, like, say, the old *Orontes* and the four Strath liners. They were killed off by new British merchant ship rules on stability, which none of them could pass. Then the cargo they had carried was now going to the first generation of more efficient container ships. They all needed expensive refits to endure. Their insurance premiums were rising. Fuel oil prices were rising. But most of all, it was the intrusion of the jumbo jet to Australia and the Pacific. I recall the *Himalaya* [with 1,450 berths] returning from Australia in the early 1970s with only 20 passengers in first class and 140 in tourist.

David Carr recalled,

I made the last voyage of the *Iberia* in the spring of 1972 and then looked after her at the Southampton Docks as the Japanese scrap merchants came aboard for inspection. Once the final deal was completed, the *Iberia* was stripped of all fittings, even down to the linens. These were put into storage at Southampton and later sold off, some to collectors.

The *Iberia* went to the breakers prematurely, in September 1972.

Iberia

30,000 TONS

Fully Air-conditioned and Stabilized

takes its name from the first scheduled service of the P&O Steam Navigation Company, carrying passengers and mail between London and the Iberian Peninsula. Built in 1954 she accommodates 651 first class and 733 tourist class passengers with a crew of 711 IBERIA cruises at 22 knots with a length of 719 feet and 91 feet breadth.

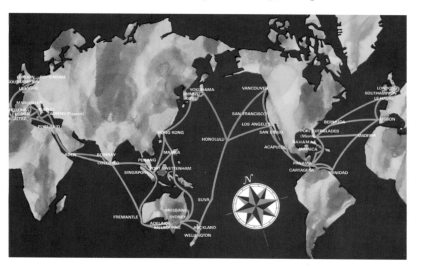

An updated global map of P&O-Orient liner services in 1970. (P&O)

DRAWING ROOM, THE MAIN LOUNGE IN FIRST CLASS, BRIGHT AND CHEERFULLY APPOINTED

BUILT FOR THE WARM WEATHER ROUTES THESE SHIPS OFFER A OF OUTDOOR RECREATION

Accommodations aboard the *Iberia*. (P&O)

Above: A superb photo: the *Iberia* outward bound from Sydney in 1972. (Author's Collection)

Above right: The *Iberia* being repaired at Garden Island, Sydney, after a collision with the tanker *Stanvac Pretoria*. The date is April 1956. (Lindsay Johnson Collection)

Right: The splendid-looking *Iberia*, dressed in flags for the occasion, arrives at New York during a three-week Atlantic cruise. The date is June 1959. (Moran Towing & Transportation Co.)

20

ORSOVA

Captain Bob Ellingham served aboard freighters until posted in 1956 to the *Orsova*, then the Orient Line flagship. Afterward, he had stints of service aboard the *Orcades*, *Empire Orwell*, *Oronsay*, *Orontes* and *Orion*. It seemed that the only Orient liner of that time was, in fact, the last ship of the fleet before its greater integration into P&O in 1960. Rather oddly, Captain Ellingham had yet to serve aboard the *Oriana*.

'The Orient Line differed from its P&O counterpart in that Orient had all-European crews,' the captain recounted.

The P&O liners had British officers and some European crew, but mostly Goans from India and lascars from Pakistan. The Orient liners were each quite superb in their design and decoration, possibly the very best on the Aussie run at the time. First-class accommodations were upper deck and forward; tourist class was aft. The tourist section was almost always fully booked by the British government for outward immigrants. It was quite rare to have any empty space. At times, this presented a problem. For example, we often put into Navarino Bay in Greece to load Greek immigrants, whose passage was being underwritten by one of the big tanker tycoons. We simply had to put them in first class. We sometimes returned with reverse immigrants – those souls, who after a year or two, did not find Australian life to their liking. Other homeward passengers included near-endless numbers of Australian tourists bound for both Britain and Europe.

The 28,790-grt *Orsova* was a modernized version of the earlier *Orcades* and *Oronsay*, but went a noticeable step further by not having a traditional mast. Rigging was attached instead to the ship's very dominant single funnel. Built by Vickers at Barrow and completed in March 1954, the 723-foot-long *Orsova* was a P&O-Orient favorite. In later years, in 1973–74, P&O actually planned to keep the *Orsova* as a cruise ship and scrap the far larger and newer *Canberra*. The *Orsova* always had great popularity, both on the liner runs and on cruises.

Howard Franklin sailed in each of the three big, post-war Orient liners. 'Orient Line ships differed from P&O ships,' he recalled.

First class aboard Orient Line ships felt like an English country house whereas P&O ships were more like hotels. Orient Line had the better food and impeccable service, far superior to P&O. First class on the Union-Castle Line was very similar to the Orient Line. It was all very formal, very exact, very Old World.

'Orient Line officers wore distinctive uniforms with high neck collars. It was all very clean cut,' added Franklin.

It was also very, very British. Traveling in first class aboard the *Orcades*, *Oronsay* and *Orsova* was a cross between a very grand hotel and an English public school. It was all very orderly, calm and precise. First class included a Silver Grill aboard each ship.

These had the most superb service and very French designated foods. All the menus were in French as well. It was quite different from P&O, from say the *Himalaya*, *Chusan*, *Arcadia* and *Iberia*. They were both utterly and completely British, but Orient Line was actually the more colonial. The Orient liners carried huge numbers of the British and Indian armies. In first class, there were top Government officials, very rich businessmen and their wives, and bejeweled maharajas with their wives, courts and entourages. The *Orcades*, *Oronsay* and *Orsova* were very comfortable ships, but were very post-Second World War minimalist. Their decor was mostly light woods, mosaics and lino flooring.

Captain Philip Jackson served aboard several of the large, P&O post-war liners, most notably the *Himalaya* and *Orsova*. 'By the early 1970s, we were faced with some major decisions. It was, for the most part, the end for many of our older, fuel-costly liners. By 1973, the *Orcades* was twenty-five, the *Orcades* reached twenty-two and the *Orsova* was almost twenty years old.'

In the care of a much reduced crew of seventy-two, the *Orsova* left Southampton for the last time on 14 December 1973. Her P&O days were all but over – she was on her way to breakers out on Taiwan.

A first-class deck plan, 1959. (Andrew Kilk Collection)

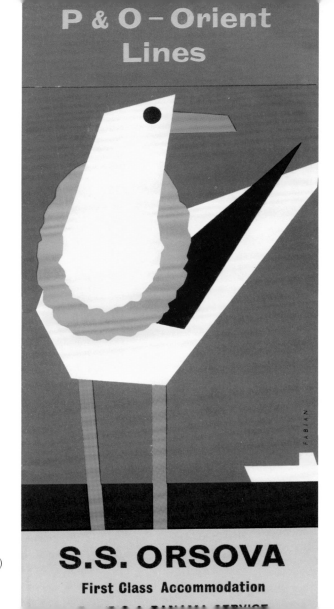

P & O – Orient Lines

FABIAN

S.S. ORSOVA

First Class Accommodation

Orsova

29,000 TONS

Fully Air-conditioned
and Stabilized

takes her name from a small town on the Danube where the rapids known as "The Iron Gate" were for centuries a barrier to ships. Built in 1954, with accommodations for 692 first class, and 811 tourist class passengers. She has a crew of 634. Speed 22 knots.
Length 723 feet—Breadth 94 feet.

Above: The innovative *Orsova* during her sea trials, when she reached a top speed of 25.58 knots. She was heralded as the fastest liner to Australia in the mid-1950s. (Cronican-Arroyo Collection)

VIEW, LOOKING AFT OF THE TOURIST CLASS SWIMMING POOL WITH SPORTS DECKS IN BACKGROUND

A POPULAR PLACE IS THIS COMFORTABLE CINEMA

Left: The beautiful *Orsova*. (P&O)

WATCHING THE SUNSET BEFORE DINNER

EACH SHIP HAS A SPACIOUS LOUNGE LIKE THIS FORWARD ON THE PROMENADE DECK FOR THE ENJOYMENT OF FIRST CLASS PASSENGERS

THIS TOURIST CLASS LOUNGE IS ALWAYS A POPULAR PART OF THE SHIP

TOURIST PASSENGERS ENJOY THIS CONGENIAL AREA

Left: Accommodations aboard the *Orsova*. (P&O)

Below: Imposing. The *Orsova* underway from Sydney. (P&O)

Above: Preparing to dock. The *Orsova* was every inch the handsome-looking liner. (Luis Miguel Correia)

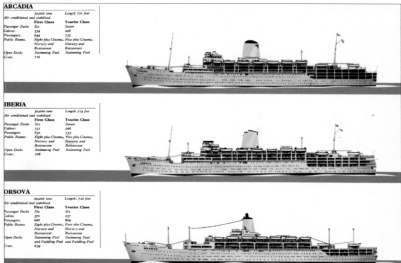

ARCADIA

	29,600 tons	Length 721 feet
Air conditioned and stabilised		
	First Class	**Tourist Class**
Passenger Decks	Six	Seven
Cabins	354	208
Passengers	644	735
Public Rooms	Eight plus Cinema, Nursery and Restaurant	Five plus Cinema, Nursery and Restaurant
Open Decks	Swimming Pool	Swimming Pool
Crew	716	

IBERIA

	30,000 tons	Length 719 feet
Air conditioned and stabilised		
	First Class	**Tourist Class**
Passenger Decks	Six	Seven
Cabins	351	206
Passengers	630	733
Public Rooms	Eight plus Cinema, Nursery and Restaurant	Five plus Cinema, Nursery and Restaurant
Open Decks	Swimming Pool	Swimming Pool
Crew	708	

ORSOVA

	29,000 tons	Length 722 feet
Air conditioned and stabilised		
	First Class	**Tourist Class**
Passenger Decks	Six	Six
Cabins	370	257
Passengers	688	809
Public Rooms	Eight plus Cinema, Nursery and Restaurant	Four plus Cinema, Nursery and Restaurant
Open Decks	Swimming Pool and Paddling Pool	Swimming Pool and Paddling Pool
Crew	639	

Left: The *Orsova* was paired with the *Arcadia* and *Iberia*. (P&O)

21

CATHAY AND *CHITRAL*

David Carr joined P&O in 1960. It was then considered a very good opportunity for a young man wanting a life at sea.

My first assignments were aboard cargo ships, but then, and quite quickly, I was lucky to get a passenger ship – the combination passenger-cargo liner *Cathay*. She was the former Belgian *Baudouinville* [built in 1956–57, her sister, the *Chitral*, had been the *Jadotville*], previously used on the colonial run to and from the Congo. The *Cathay* was like a private yacht – 13,800 tons and carrying up to 231 passengers, all of them in first class. She was also a very fine 'sea boat'. We had ten-week round trips: out from London and then Southampton, through the Med and Suez, and then onto Singapore, Hong Kong, Kobe and Yokohama. We would carry lots of service people – the Hong Kong police and civil servants, for example. We used the old King George V – the 'KGV' – Dock at London and had a two-week turnaround there. It seems so improbable by today's rapid, overnight containership standards. After London, we stopped briefly at Southampton. Passengers would have an easier train ride down from London.

Of course, cargo was very important to a ship like the *Cathay* [and *Chitral*]. Outwards, we carried lots of general cargo, which often included crated automobiles. Homebound, there was more general cargo, but most of it was for Woolworths in Britain. This included umbrellas, toys and mostly inexpensive plastic items. On the homeward voyages, Woolworths reserved at least one full hatch.

Captain Philip Jackson also served in *Chitral*. He recalled,

I served as the chief officer and therefore looked after the 240 all-first-class passengers. Eight [hours] out of my ten-hour days were spent in planning and organizing passenger entertainment. The quartermaster served as my assistant, the daytime children's attendant alternated as my night-time hostess and otherwise there was a three-piece band. We'd have deck games and sports, late afternoon bingo, concerts and the occasional cinema presentation. Because of the small numbers, the entire ship had something of a private yacht atmosphere. Older, well-heeled passengers loved a ship like the *Chitral* and her sister, the *Cathay*. The Sultan of Selangor often traveled with us, taking ten–fifteen cabins for his entourage, for shopping trips from Singapore to Hong Kong and return.

The *Cathay* and *Chitral* were P&O's last passenger ships on the UK–Far East run. They were transferred over to the Eastern & Australian Steamship Company Limited in 1969–70 and were used for a time on the Australia–Far East route. Soon outmoded in this service, the *Chitral* was scrapped in 1976; the *Cathay* was sold to the Chinese, becoming the *Shanghai* for Shanghai–Hong Kong service until scrapped in 1996.

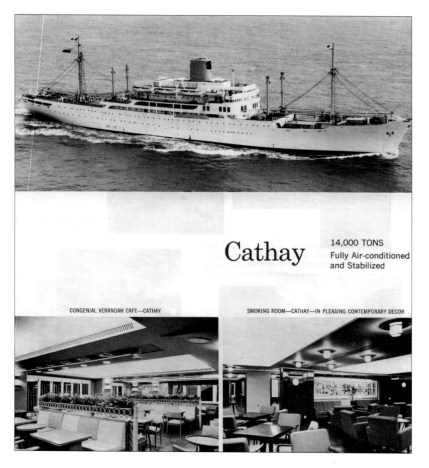

Cathay

14,000 TONS
Fully Air-conditioned
and Stabilized

CONGENIAL VERANDAH CAFE—CATHAY

SMOKING ROOM—CATHAY—IN PLEASING CONTEMPORARY DECOR

Accommodations aboard the *Cathay*. (P&O)

Classic lines. The beautiful-looking *Cathay* seen at Southampton in 1968. (B. Reeves)

TWIN BED
CABIN
WITH
BATHROOM

Below: The *Chitral* had been the Belgian Line's *Jadotville*, used on the Antwerp–Congo run. (Alex Duncan)

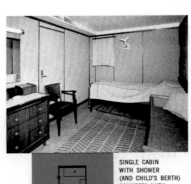

SINGLE CABIN
WITH SHOWER
(AND CHILD'S BERTH)
CONNECTS WITH
ADJOINING CABIN

DOUBLE CABIN
(UPPER & LOWER)
WITH SHOWER

Passenger quarters aboard the high-standard, all-first-class *Cathay* and *Chitral*. (P&O)

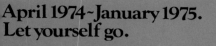

April 1974~January 1975.
Let yourself go.

Member of the

P&O

Group

Meander your way through the East aboard yacht-like E&A Cathay or Chitral.

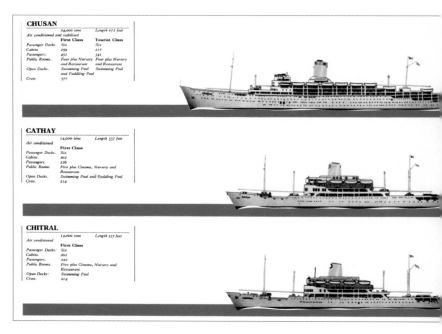

Above: The *Cathay* and *Chitral* were paired with the *Chusan* on the UK–Far East run in the 1960s. (P&O)

Left: The *Cathay* and *Chitral* served on the Eastern & Australian Line's Australia–Far East service in the 1970s. (Andrew Kilk Collection)

22

ORIANA

'The *Oriana* was an outstanding ship. She was a traditional ocean liner,' recalled Captain Ian Tompkins. 'Myself, I always felt that the Orient Line made superb, often superior ships.'

Just as P&O and the Orient Line began to merge their liner sailings in 1954, both companies saw great promise in the future of liner travel, especially expanded, worldwide liner travel. Consequently, both companies turned their attention to planning their largest, finest and fastest liners yet. Orient Line followed up with designs of the *Orsova* of 1954 and reworked and enhanced them to produce the radically different *Oriana*, launched at Barrow on 3 November 1959, with a royal sponsor: Princess Alexandra of Kent. Initially designed as a single-stacker, a ventilator placed further aft and lower appears to be a second funnel. Like the *Orsova*, the actual funnel is high and dominant, and gives the ship an important as well as powerful stance. In fact, during her sea trials in the fall of 1960, the 804-footer reached an astounding 30.64 knots. She was the fastest British liner since the Cunard Queens of the 1930s. She would cut the Southampton–Sydney journey to twenty-one days, a great selling point to business passengers.

Both as a passenger and later as a guest speaker, Howard Franklin sailed the *Oriana* on numerous occasions. '*Oriana* was quite different, especially in first class, from *Canberra*,' he recalled.

The *Oriana* was, it seemed, all graciousness and luxury, and lots of carpets whereas the *Canberra* was more informal and had acres of lino flooring. I was always amazed with the low ceilings in the tourist-class public rooms aboard *Canberra* and by the smaller, even tiny cabins. As built, the *Oriana* also had a Silver Grill up in first class, but this was later removed and made into cabins. The Monkey Bar was a favorite of mine. You felt like you were suspended over the ocean itself. There was also an enormous proportion of drinks. The *Oriana* also had a wonderful enclosed promenade area. There was, it seemed, always greater excitement on sailing day in the *Oriana*. There were lots of reunions and meetings with regular passengers. The commodore of the Orient Line would be aboard and, as I recall, he was a very precise, very exacting man.

In August 1970, the *Oriana* made headlines – she had a fire just after sailing from Southampton. 'I was working for the World Health Organization in Geneva and decided to "blow everything" and go on home leave to San Francisco in the *Oriana*,' remembered Elinor Kamath.

I bought 'sun clothes' for the three-week trip [via the Caribbean and Panama] and even had my hair cut short so I could swim. I had splendid ideas, but two hours out of Southampton we were on fire. Smoke billowed from the ship. It was all very dramatic, very serious. We were worried. A small tourist plane from the Isle of Wight was quickly flying nearby with a banner 'See the *Oriana* on fire!' even before the first fireboat arrived from the refinery nearby. We quickly realized that you can be in as much trouble in sight of shore as anywhere on the seas!

'We went eventually to dry-dock in Southampton,' added Mrs Kamath.

I eventually got shore permission and staggered into the local hotel I'd left in excitement the day before. P&O evidently had the same trouble, another fire, with the *Oriana* in Fiji six months before, but they had it hushed up. They spent a long time before they sailed, having to haul all the Australia-bound emigrants off the ship day after day to sightsee and be fed so repairs could be done.

Captain Nick Carlton joined P&O in 1970 and within two years was posted to the company's second largest liner, the 41,000-grt *Oriana*. 'Everything was just about changing when I joined her,' he recalled.

We were doing less and less line voyages. The £10 migrant era was winding down. Instead, we did more and more cruising – even as many as a dozen cruises from Sydney with Australians. It was two-class cruising. We even switched to the Australian dollar as the onboard currency. It was all changing on these cruises. It was bare feet on formal night!

'The *Oriana* was a great "sea boat", making 27 knots as a normal service speed,' recalled Captain Carlton. 'She had done 33 knots on her trials back in 1960 and could still make 30 knots when needed. She was a very impressive looking ship, in ways a "real ship".'
According to Captain Nick Carlton,

the *Oriana* was always friendlier and had better itineraries as a cruise ship than the *Canberra*. Many thought that the *Canberra*, being the P&O flagship, was snobby. We used to call it *Canberra-*

itis! There is [sic] always differences between ships. Later, at P&O, it was often said that the *Pacific Princess* was friendlier and had better onboard chemistry than her sister ship, the *Island Princess*. Sometimes, the captain of a ship sets the tone and that can affect a ship's chemistry. As cruise ships, we often thought the *Canberra* had the more boring cruises – to Vigo, Tenerife, the Med. Alternately, the *Oriana* did more diverse cruises – the North Cape, the Baltic, Caribbean, even the USA.

'The 1970s, especially the early 1970s, were critical times at P&O,' recalled Captain Philip Jackson.

Ships such as the *Oriana* and *Canberra* of 1960–61 were built primarily for our fast UK–Australia run and for migrants. Then, quite suddenly and most dramatically, Mr Boeing's jumbo jets appeared in regions east of the Suez. We abruptly lost the bulk of our trade. Our passengers were sent roving around the world – and more often to North American shores – looking for business. In fact, the older liners such as the *Orcades* and *Chusan* were soon sent off to the junkyards of Taiwan. Their good life's work, their economic well-being, had ended. We formed P&O Cruises in 1973 and converted the *Oriana* and *Canberra* to one class. They became all but full-time cruise ships. Although the official class barriers on board disappeared, we found that in most ways these ships remained socially separate. We probably never needed the partitions in the first place.

In late 1981, the *Oriana* left Southampton and the UK forever. She was to be a full-time cruise ship sailing from Sydney. 'I attended the farewell luncheon onboard,' added Howard Franklin. 'Princess Alexandra attended as well and had a last look over the ship. I always felt the *Oriana* didn't convert to one class for cruising as well as the *Canberra*. *Canberra* was a better one-class ship.'

I cruised with Captain Philip Jackson on a fifteen-night voyage from Sydney in July 1984. At the time, he said,

At the age of twenty-four, I believe that *Oriana* can look forward to several further years on the Australian cruise run. [The rumor was that she would last until late 1987.] Recently, we've made some alterations – such as reducing her cruise capacity from 1,750 to 1,550 and the total staff from 790 to 690. Next year [1985], she'll have a $12-million, two-week refit at Singapore. We have a 30 per cent repeat passenger factor here in Australia, but we feel there is a huge untapped market. Ideally, we need to go to new South Pacific ports, but then with such a big liner as *Oriana*, we are obviously quite limited when considering anchorages, depths and wharf conditions. Recently, we strengthened our onboard entertainment program with added special theme cruises – such as the Variety Club and Melbourne Cup cruises – and hope to tap into the opening of the big Australian convention trade.

Plans changed, however. The *Oriana* was retired from P&O service in the spring of 1986 and was sold to Japanese buyers, who had the liner towed to Beppu on Kyushu Island for use as a hotel, entertainment centre and museum. Less than successful, she was sold to Chinese buyers in 1995 and towed to Qinhuandao and then, in 1998, to Shanghai. She changed locations once more, in 2000, when she was shifted to Dalien. Finally, she seemed successful, but then, in June 2004, was ripped from her moorings and capsized during a huge storm. Refloated a year later, she was not worthy of repairs and was towed away to Zhangiagang to be scrapped.

The bulbous bow of the 804-foot-long *Oriana* is seen in this dry dock view at Falmouth. (P&O)

Tasmanian Devilled Eggs   Smoked Salmon
Queensland Pineapple Cocktail with Pernod

\# \# \#

Captain Cook's Broth   Kangaroo Tail Soup

\# \# \#

King Prawns, Rottnest Island
Chicken, Hunter Valley Style

Baked Ham Jubilee

Fillet of Beef, Strathaird

\# \# \#

Sugared Pumpkin   Minted Green Peas
Potatoes: Roast   Boiled   Creamed

\# \# \#

Cold Buffet: Assorted Cold Cuts
Surfer's Paradise Salad
Tossed Green Salad

ss Strathaird

50 Years of P&O Cruising — 1932-1982

GOLDEN ANNIVERSARY DINNER

On board ss Oriana, 18 December, 1982

Above: An anniversary dinner menu cover celebrating fifty years of P&O cruising in Australia. (P&O)

Left: The celebratory luncheon aboard the *Oriana* at Sydney, 18 December 1982. (P&O)

Above: Underneath the *Oriana* in the King George V Graving Dock at Southampton. (P&O)

Top right: The mighty 41,000-grt *Oriana* arriving at Southampton. (P&O)

Right: The two biggest P&O-Orient liners: the *Canberra* and *Oriana*. (P&O)

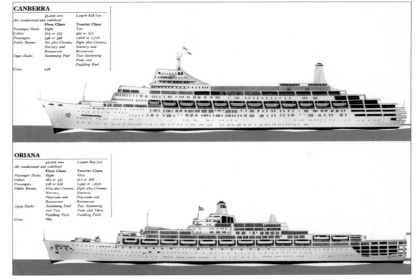

Oriana

42,000 TONS

Fully Air-conditioned and Stabilized

was the name given Queen Elizabeth I by poets when she ruled England over 400 years ago. ORIA[NA] built in 1960 during the second Elizabethan era. She accommodates 630 first class and 1476 tourist c[lass] passengers and a crew of 900 She is 804 feet long, 97 feet wide and has a speed of 27½ knots.

ALCOVES AND TABLES LINE THE DANCE FLOOR OF THE TOURIST CLASS BALLROOM

PRINCESS ROOM THE MAGNIFICENT FIRST CLASS LOUNGE

The exciting *Oriana*! (Andrew Kilk Collection)

Accommodations aboard the popular *Oriana*. (P&O)

FIRST CLASS
PASSENGERS ENJOYING
A DELIGHTFUL MEAL

DECK TENNIS ON ONE OF THE VAST SPORTS DECKS

FIRST CLASS SWIMMING POOL—TOURIST CLASS HAS TWO

MIDSHIP BAR
THE ATMOSPHERE
SPEAKS FOR ITSELF

Some P&O passengers preferred the *Oriana* over the *Canberra*. (P&O)

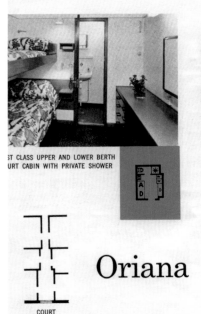

ST CLASS UPPER AND LOWER BERTH
URT CABIN WITH PRIVATE SHOWER

FIRST CLASS
DELUXE CABIN
TWO BEDS WITH
PRIVATE BATHROOM

COURT

Oriana

is an efficient performing ship—holder of every speed record between Gibralter and North America via Suez With adjustable air-conditioning, each first class cabin has a private bath or shower and toilet, telephones, two stationed, individually controlled music system and running ice water Many inside cabins have been brilliantly arranged around courts with large windows overlooking the sea. Each "court cabin" has a window which looks out to the ocean beyond the court.

FIRST CLASS TWO BERTH OUTSIDE CABIN WITH PRIVATE BATHROOM

OUTSIDE SINGLE BERTH CABIN IN FIRST CLASS WITH SH

First-class cabins aboard the *Oriana*. (P&O)

Above: Arrival at Suva, on Fiji, one of *Oriana*'s many ports of call. (P&O)

Top left: Night-time splendor at Sydney. The *Oriana* rests at Circular Quay between voyages. (P&O)

Left: Rare meeting at San Francisco. The *Oriana* remains at berth as the *Canberra* departs. (P&O)

During her first visit to New York in August 1979, the *Oriana* made the front page of *Towline*, the magazine of Moran Towing. (Moran Towing Towing & Transportation Co.)

The *Oriana* in dry dock at Singapore. (P&O)

Above: Arriving in New York for the first time in August 1979 – the author is on the far right, waving from the starboard bridge wing. (David Edwardsen)

Left: Celebrity passengers, Cary Grant and his wife Dyan Cannon with their seven-month-old daughter Jennifer, aboard the *Oriana* during a Trans-Canal cruise in July 1966. (Ginger Fortin)

Above: Departing Sydney in January 1986. (Lindsay Johnson Collection)

Top right: Maiden arrival at San Francisco, 1961. (P&O)

Right: A new style of advertising for P&O cruising by the late 1960s. (Author's Collection)

Above: Off and away as the *Oriana* passes under Sydney Harbour Bridge on 14 February 1986. (Lindsay Johnson Collection)

Top right: Laid up at Pyrmont, Sydney, and soon to be towed to Japan. (Lindsay Johnson Collection)

Right: The *Oriana* moored at Beppu, Japan, in 1987. (Author's Collection)

23

CANBERRA

Tremendous interest in P&O was created in the early 1960s as the *Oriana* and *Canberra* came into service. They were largest and fastest liners to be built for a service other than the North Atlantic. They were also the biggest British-flag liners since the *Queen Elizabeth* of 1940. The *Canberra*, built by Harland & Wolff at Belfast and commissioned in the spring of 1961, was not, however, without her problems. David Carr recalled her early woes:

At her launching at Belfast in March 1960, it was found she was lower in the stern than planned. What a shocking – and embarrassing – dilemma! A counter action was needed and so cement was placed in the bow. Now, instead of 32 feet, she drew 35 feet of water. It seems that Belfast-built liners had stability problems. The *Iberia* [1954] had such problems all of her life whereas her sister, the *Arcadia* [John Brown-built at Clydebank], had none.

The 818-foot-long *Canberra* – the biggest liner ever for Australian service – was delivered in June 1961. Immediately, she was a newsworthy and popular ship. But there were some teething problems of a kind. 'Of course, *Canberra*'s biggest problem – and blemish – was her engine breakdown off Malta and while outbound for Australia in January 1963,' added David Carr.

The homeward-bound *Strathmore* was nearby and offered her a tow, but *Canberra* refused. Instead, *Strathmore* ferried over food in lifeboats. Actually, I believe *Strathmore* was on her very last P&O voyage at the time. *Canberra* eventually returned to Southampton and then to her builders at Belfast for repairs.

'I remember the *Canberra* as darker, almost oppressive in some areas for a modern ship,' recalled Howard Franklin.

She lacked light, either natural or artificial, as I remember. Myself, I was never quite impressed by *Canberra*, but many, many people liked, even loved her, and were very sentimental about her following the Falklands. She had, however, great innovation at P&O with her court cabins. I felt the Century Bar was the best on the ship, a sort of secret hideaway. I remember that the Meridian Room was called 'God's Waiting Room'. Everyone seemed to sleep there, but some never awoke. Some also called it the 'Mortician's Salon'. The *Canberra* also had an interesting crew and, amongst the waiters and bedroom stewards, these included some larger-than-life characters.

In the summer of 1988, we cruised aboard the four-year-old, 44,000-grt *Royal Princess*. Captain Ian Tompkins compared her to the innovative, but earlier *Canberra*. 'Like the *Canberra* in her time, the *Royal Princess* is light years ahead of other P&O-Princess liners. The two ships differed, however, in some ways. The *Royal Princess* was superbly successful, operationally brilliant, more precise than any P&O liner of recent memory.'

Times continued to change, of course. 'The serang was an Indian boatswain and was like a king to our Bombay deck crews.

These serangs were the very best,' recalled Captain Tompkins. 'The last of these finished in the *Canberra* in 1986–87. These days, we have all Pakistani deck crews.'

After going to the South Atlantic in the Falklands war in 1982, the *Canberra* returned as a heroic ship and seemed to enjoy a renewed, even new, popularity. She sailed on for another fifteen years. Her final cruise came in September 1997. She had sailed for thirty-six years. Her very last voyage was to the breakers at Gadani Beach in Pakistan. She arrived there on 28 October, was deliberately beached and then invaded by the demolition crews.

A preliminary model of the *Canberra*, 1957. (Richard Faber Collection)

Launch of   **2361**

S.S. "CANBERRA"

by

DAME PATTIE MENZIES, G.B.E.

on Wednesday, 16th March, 1960.

ADMIT ONE PERSON

TO MUSGRAVE SHIPYARD

Ticket holders should arrive at No. 14 Slipway, Musgrave Shipyard, Hamilton Road, not later than 12 - 00 noon.

THIS CARD MUST BE SHOWN ON REQUEST

Admission to the naming ceremonies. (Author's Collection)

Opposite page: Ready for launching. The *Canberra* at Belfast, 16 March 1961. (P&O)

Above: A dramatic view of the upper, open decks from the ship's mast. (P&O)

Left: The splendid *Canberra* underway. (P&O)

P&O *Ships of the Fleet*

Cunard Line Ltd. is the General Agent for P&O's Canberra
in the United States.

P&O

CUNARD

Your Run Away to Sea Resorts

P&O was represented by Cunard when the *Canberra* cruised from New York for nine months in 1973. (P&O)

Canberra was flagship to P&O's 'Ships of the Fleet'. (P&O)

Canberra

45,000 TONS
Fully Air-conditioned and Stabilized

takes her name in honor of the capital city of Australia, is an aboriginal word meaning "place by the water" or meeting place. Known as the ship that shapes the future, CANBERRA was built in 1961, cruises at 27½ knots, has accommodations for 598 first class and 1590 tourist class and 1000 crew She is fitted with transverse propulsion equipment is 818 feet in length with a breadth of 102 feet.

THERE ARE CHILDREN'S PLAYROOM FACILITIES FOR EACH CLASS WITH SUPERVISED PLAY BY TRAINED ENGLISH NANNIES

THE MERIDIAN ROOM, BEAUTIFULLY MODERN FIRST CLASS LOUNGE

Accommodations aboard the 44,807-grt *Canberra*. (P&O)

TOP RIGHT
THE FIRST CLASS RESTAURANT IS ON TWO
LEVELS AND SOFTLY LIT FOR PLEASANT DINING

2nd FROM TOP
WILLIAM FAWCETT ROOM EVER POPULAR
TOURIST CLASS LOUNGE

3rd FROM TOP RIGHT
THE ALICE SPRINGS ROOM OVERLOOKS
ONE OF THE TWO SWIMMING POOLS
AVAILABLE IN TOURIST CLASS

BOTTOM RIGHT
THE TOURIST CLASS RESTAURANT
IS INFORMAL AND RESTFUL IN DECOR

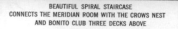

BEAUTIFUL SPIRAL STAIRCASE
CONNECTS THE MERIDIAN ROOM WITH THE CROWS NEST
AND BONITO CLUB THREE DECKS ABOVE

Splendor at sea – quarters aboard the *Canberra*. (P&O)

Canberra's maiden arrival at New York in June 1962. (Port Authority of New York & New Jersey)

Artist Don Stoltenberg's stylized salute to the P&O flagship. (Author's Collection)

Canberra at Sydney in February 1964. (P&O)

Heroic return. The huge welcome for the *Canberra* when she returned to Southampton from the Falklands War in 1982. (P&O)

Oriana and *Canberra* together at Southampton on 3 September 1964. (H. J. Wood)

The *Canberra* was the largest liner ever to visit Japan when she called at Yokohama on 15 March 1966. The *George Anson* and *Sagafjord* are on the outer side of the port's South Pier; the *Chitral* is berthed on the right, just ahead of the *Canberra*. (P&O)

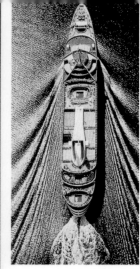

CANBERRA
Farewell Cruise
10th – 30th September 1997

Postcard commemorating the final cruise, 10–30 September 1997. (P&O)

Right: Canberra deck plan, dated August 1963. (Andrew Kilk Collection)

Next page: Her last arrival in San Francisco on 14 March 1997. (Marvin Jensen)

P&O-ORIENT LINES

SS **CANBERRA**

AUGUST 1963

FIRST CLASS

Changing times! The *Canberra* meets the brand-new *Royal Princess* at Southampton in the fall of 1984. (P&O)

Celebrations! For the fiftieth anniversary celebrations of the D-Day Landings in June 1994, the *Canberra* is joined by countless craft including the royal yacht *Britannia* and the *Queen Elizabeth 2*. (P&O)

Two icons in Australia: the *Canberra* and the Sydney Opera House. (Lindsay Johnson Collection)

Canberra's triumphant if sentimental return to Southampton following her farewell cruise. (Clive Harvey)

AFTERWORD – P&O AND PRINCESS CRUISES

'We built the *Spirit of London* [1972] as our bid to move into cruising, especially North American cruising,' recalled Captain Bob Ellingham.

I was transferred to the Los Angeles offices of Princess Cruises, a company that we bought [in 1974] so as to expand more rapidly. At first, however, we worked as P&O Lines. We developed a rather good following with the *Spirit of London*, and intended to acquire two more cruise ships, the Norwegian *Sea Venture* and *Island Venture*, which were to become the *Spirit of Liverpool* and *Spirit of Southampton*. P&O wanted to model their cruise division after the then new Royal Caribbean Lines of Miami. They used the name *Song of Norway* for their first ship and so we used *Spirit of London*. It was a new age for passenger ships and so new identities. Old ways and names were being pushed aside to an extent. But then we acquired Princess Cruises from Mr Stanley McDonald of Seattle and we realized Princess had an even stronger following. Consequently, we adopted the Princess concept – the *Spirit of London* became the *Sun Princess*, the *Island Venture* as the *Island Princess* and, subsequently best known of all, the *Sea Venture* as *Pacific Princess*. The very popular television series *The Love Boat* was first filmed on the *Sun Princess* [in 1975], but then quickly moved to the *Pacific Princess*. For the next dozen or so years, the *Pacific Princess* was just about a household name. Lots and lots of people wanted to sail in her, hoping the TV cast and stars would be aboard. Many volunteered to be 'extras' in the filming sequences. That series turned out to be a stroke of genius. It turned Princess Cruises into a major cruise line, but also greatly helped the competition as well.

After P&O bought Los Angeles-based Princess Cruises, the future of passenger ship travel was in cruising. The era of line voyages was all but over. P&O Cruises had the *Canberra* and *Oriana* in UK-based cruising by then and the older, but still popular, *Arcadia* running full-time cruises from Australia. Sweden's *Kungsholm* was later added, becoming the *Sea Princess*. She would later join the *Canberra* in UK cruising while the *Oriana* replaced the *Arcadia* out in Australia. By the mid-1980s, a host of newly built ships followed, beginning with the 44,000-grt *Royal Princess* of 1984. These days, by 2014, P&O Cruises is the biggest cruise operator in the UK market, the second-largest in the world after the US trade. Sister company Princess has over two dozen cruise liners and P&O Australia has a half-dozen. The market is huge – and filled with further growth.

While those bygone P&O liners, such as the *Stratheden*, *Himalaya*, *Orsova* and *Canberra*, are now gone, their legacies live on in today's vast cruise industry. More people are traveling on ships than ever before. And so, as the P&O slogan once noted, it is still 'Runaway to sea'!

P&O-Orient posters of the 1950s and 1960s. (Author's Collection)

"A Run Away to Sea Adventure"

ORIENT

float or fly

orient

LINE

Sea/Air Return Tickets to and from the Mediterranean

This image and the following: Orontes, Orcades, Himalaya, Chusan, Oronsay, Iberia, Arcadia, Chitral, Oriana and *Canberra*. (Author's Collection)

BIBLIOGRAPHY

Dunn, Laurence, *Passenger Liners*. London: Adlard Coles Ltd, 1961.

Dunn, Laurence, *Passenger Liners*. London: Adlard Coles Ltd, 1965.

Heine, Frank and Lose, Frank, *Great Passenger Ships of the World*. Hamburg, Germany: Koehlers Verlagsgesellschaft, 2010.

Kludas, Arnold, *Great Passenger Ships of the World: Vol. 4, 1936–50*. Cambridge, England: Patrick Stephens Ltd, 1977.

Kludas, Arnold, *Great Passenger Ships of the World: Vol. 5, 1951–76*. Cambridge, England: Patrick Stephens Ltd, 1977.

Lunn, Geoff, *And the Crew Went Too: The 10 Pound Assisted Passage*. Stroud, England: Tempus Publishing, 2007.

Mayes, William, *Cruise Ships* (Fourth Edition). Windsor, England: Overview Press Ltd, 2011.

Miller, William H. and Noble, Tim, *East of Suez: Liners to Australia in the 1950s & 1960s*. Stroud, England: Amberley Publishing, 2013.

Miller, William H., *Great American Passenger Ships*. Stroud, England: The History Press Ltd, 2012.

Miller, William H., *Greek Passenger Liners*. Stroud, England: Tempus Publishing Ltd, 2006.

Miller, William H., *Pictorial Encyclopedia of Ocean Liners, 1860–1994*. Mineola, New York: Dover Publications Inc., 1995.

Miller, William H., *Under the Red Ensign: British Passenger Ships of the 1950s & 1960s*. Stroud, England: The History Press, 2009.

Plowman, Peter, *Australian Cruise Ships*. Dural Delivery Center, New South Wales: Rosenberg Publishing Pty Ltd, 2007.

Plowman, Peter, *Australian Migrant Ships 1946–77*. Dural Delivery Center, New South Wales: Rosenburg Publishing Pty Ltd, 2006.

Plowman, Peter, *Coast to Coast: The Great Australian Coastal Liners*. Dural Delivery Center, New South Wales: Rosenberg Publishing Pty Ltd, 2007.

Ocean & Cruise News (1980–2014). Northport, New York: World Ocean & Cruise Liner Society.

Official Steamship Guide (1951–63). New York City: Transportation Guides Inc.